MW01354354

Daily Direction For Ladies & Mothers, Witches & others

*Suzie Newell, D.N.P.*
*And the Gnostic Sentries*

ISBN: 978-0-578-87990-1

Please reach out to Foxglove Studios for more information regarding sales and distribution of this book and related material.
www.Foxgloveartists.com

MANIFEST

*Suzie Newell and the Gnostic Sentries*

First and foremost, this is a collaborative project of six highly driven and artistic individuals without whom, I would have been lost. When working toward my doctorate at the University of Cincinnati we had the revolutionary idea that my work with women with substance use disorder should be available to everyone. I had developed a program that focused on coping mechanisms for women. This work and my experience with peer support weren't exclusively for women with a diagnosis, but rather, could apply to anyone. So, I wrote the book. Then I called upon the amazingly talented people in my life to make it a work of art, an app, an audiobook— a treasure trove of resources. In our initial meeting, through a bit of spiritual digging, we landed on the idea of Gnosis (meaning knowledge of spiritual mysteries) as a guiding theme. The Gnostic Sentries were born!

*Eyes burning and searching*
*The weight of the pack crushes her shoulders*
*Each step brings more pain*
*The Journey is long*

*Sunlight patches tinted green*
*Through a verdant canopy*
*Distant water falling over rocks*
*Wind mists across skin*
*Skin that sparkles with the dew of effort*
*Tiny purple flowers sprinkle the edges*
*Creating fragrance and art and splendor*
*This Path is beautiful*

*Trudging, choosing, moving forward*
*Breathing, believing, becoming*
*Working, resting, moving toward*
*An inner peaceful thrumming*

*Chirping birds*
*Unseen creatures snapping branches*
*So much beauty, so much pain*
*She walks*
*She stumbles*
*She sees*
*She trips*
*She falls*
*She breathes*
*She laughs*
*She learns*
*She chooses*

*And by choosing her own Path*
*She becomes*
*The woman she was meant to be.*

# Introduction

*How Do I Read This Book, Suze?*

Like a girl on a mission and read it straight through? Or, do I savor all the bits?

The book builds on itself. In other words, it was designed to be read in order. But, as you will learn: we don't judge here.

The book is divided into 28 sections. All told, there are 365 directions. (The 366th is a bonus message). Each message has a title, a tag line, a message, and an intention. The title is obvious (usually). The message is the message. And the intention is designed as a question so that you can create your own intention, or focus, for the day. This intention or focus is all dependent on where you are and what you need that day. The tag line is either a quote, a summary, a commentary, or often it is my imaginary friend saying things like *"How do I read this book, Suze?"* And usually, the message will answer her concern.

*So, How do I read this book?*

There are so many ways to tackle this.

Just read one a day. This is the most straight forward answer.
But you could also,
read the whole book in one setting.
Read two a day: one in the morning and one at night.
You could read a themed section each day and journal about some of the intentions that resonated with you.

You could even, read the whole book in a week. Then, get the app and listen to one each day to-or-from wherever.

Do you hate being told how to do something?
Flip it open and read what you fancy.

# Notes On 'The Path' And 'The Journey'

*We use the term Path and Journey a lot.*

Here is how these terms are used:

Everyone is on a Journey. (Feel free to groan here).
The Journey is the walk we are on that is necessary.
In essence, it is life.

The Path represents the *choices* you make on your Journey.
Sometimes we all suck at choosing the right Path,
and that is part of this too.

Often these choices seem small.
But in your day to day life,
the small habit of choosing compassion over resentment,
willingness over avoidance, and self-love over anything
can surmount to endless possibilities.

The Path 365 is essentially a tool
to help you choose Paths that work for you;
coping mechanisms and ideals that fit your life and beliefs.

All Paths teach you something.
We don't care how you get there,
as long as you are on the Path.

# Gratitude

## 1. Be On A Journey

*Take a deep breath. Clear off your table. Clear your mind.*

What if the goal IS to Journey?

Simply step on the Path.
There is no need to be perfect.
You are where you need to be;
you are stepping on the Path.
There is no failure,
there is only the Journey.
Don't commit to winning.
Commit to trying. Commit to curiosity.
Commit to seeing the world for its possibilities.
Commit to a Journey. That is the win.
Transformation isn't a goal. It's a process.
Take a deep breath because you are already here.

Sound complicated?

That's why you take a deep breath!

Intention:
What possibilities exist for me
if I get out of the way and get on the Path?

## 2. Get Into The Flow

When you swept off that table –
you swept away any Resistance.

Fighting isn't winning.
If we find ourselves fighting everyone and everything,
we are only fighting ourselves.

Great social and spiritual leaders preach peace and joy.
Ghandi said we should be the change we want to see.
The Bible tells us to do unto others
as you would have done unto you.
Eastern philosophers tell us to be kind whenever possible.
And then remind us that it is, indeed, always possible.

Mother Jones tells us that reformation,
like education,
is a Journey, not a destination.
The same holds true for your own revolution.
The Journey is the goal: not being right,
not showing someone else that you're right.
This isn't the goal.
This only makes us tired.
Walking your own Journey and becoming the woman
you are meant to be,
*that* will change more minds than constantly fighting.
When you are committed to yourself
as fiercely as you are committed to fighting...

...you will finally be free to discover
who you are truly meant to be.

Intention:
What conflict is blocking you?
Is it a deep fear?

# 3. Open Your Heart

Compassion is Revolutionary

In order to heal from our history of trauma or abuse
we have to be open.
The anxiety and pain are by-products of fighting.
The internal war we feel flares up when we are shut down,
living in fear, and listening to that voice in our heads.

Tell that bitch to shut the hell up.
She isn't welcome here.

Now, let something else flow in;
let it replace the constant negativity.
Compassion for yourself and others is a good place to start.
It softens the edges; begins the healing.
Picture your heart as a vessel,
and pour only elixir from the Fountain of Life into it.
Clean out all the pain and negativity.
You are on the Journey and you no longer do "bad" things.
Being wrong is natural.
You learn how to improve and move forward.
This is only possible if you are willing to learn,
willing to be open to all the possibilities,
willing to take that leap of faith.

... And be Honest with yourself.

Intention:
What negativity keeps your heart
from truly opening to others?

# 4. Write It Down

This is how we heal & move forward on the Path.

Let's be honest.
No, really, let's start to look at ourselves in an honest way.
If we are starting down this Path,
it is important to be okay with being wrong.
It is also important to celebrate who we are;
The good the bad and the ugly.

The combination of all our beauty, quirks,
and good and bad habits make us uniquely who we are;
that is an amazing thing!

Use a journal, or notes app, or a video log.
Or whatever kind of log, blog, or vlog you prefer.
As long as you tell your story.

Then...
go back to it; tell it again.
Go back and make sure you include
not only the amazing stuff, but the uncomfortable stuff as well.
You are here on this Path
because you have both failed and succeeded.
Without failure there is no growth, so don't punish yourself.

Remember—tell that voice in your head to shut the hell up!

Intention:
Do I have the courage to write my story?

## 5. Practice Trust

*Share your story with someone.*

Neverrrr!

Well, sorry to say, while it's important to be honest with ourselves, it doesn't mean much if we are not also accountable.

You don't have to share every detail of your life with everyone. Practice trusting one person at a time.

Share your story with a friend or a counselor,
even if it seems scary, stretch your capactiy to share your truth.

Are we sensing a theme here?

If that sounds daunting,
maybe join an online women's group and start there.
However you decide, share and be honest.

You practiced hard to write that story,
now practice hard to tell it truthfully.
Then... do it. Tell your truth!

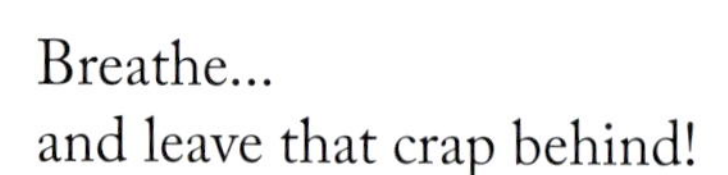

Breathe...
and leave that crap behind!

Intention:
How can I learn to trust other women?
Where do women I admire find support? Will I let myself trust?

# 6. Keep The Garden Clean

Weed out the traits
that don't belong on this journey.

You are on the path now.
You are moving through the Journey.
It's time to start eliminating what isn't useful anymore.

In your story,
you likely discovered a few things
that you don't like about yourself.
We are Journeying now,
so this isn't a bad thing.
It's a rockin' opportunity to Grow!
Sit with one of those weeds
and begin to understand
how you can eliminate it from your garden.
Then, practice it.
Will you be perfect at it tomorrow? Nope.
Get comfortable with that
and keep trying.

This is about the goal
of becoming the woman you are meant to be.
The Journey is the only thing, not perfection.
So keep trying this project of becoming.
One day you can look back after trying this daily
and be amazed at how far you have come.
But that isn't the goal, the goal is to keep trying.

Intention:
What don't I like about my garden?

# 7. Fighting Others Is Fighting The Flow

Recognize when you are Fighting yourself.

When you are angry at someone else,
you are not seeing the problem clearly.
You have zero control over their life.
What *feeds* this anger?
What possible vulnerability is hiding beneath this anger?
What insecurity allows this fight to continue?
If you didn't have a vested piece of yourself in this fight,
it wouldn't be so important,
and it wouldn't make you so angry.

What is it that makes you fight so hard?
The other person is irrelevant to your happiness.

*Maya Angelou said,*
*"It's one of the greatest gifts you can give yourself, to forgive.*
*Forgive everybody."*

Believe this with your heart and soul.
Understand that your insecurities and fears
are all tangled up in that fighting.
By giving up the fight,
you give in to peace,
so you can truly start down the Path.

The Journey is the goal.

Intention:
What am I hiding from in my anger?

## 8. Breathe

Really, breathe, like a swelling pop music melody.

Seriously! Breathe! Right now!
Begin to practice focusing on your Breathing.
When things are difficult and you can't seem to slow your mind,
you always have to Breathe.
Breathing is the one thing you have with you at all times
and that you must do at all times.
Start with a simple three minutes.

Deep breath.

Feel the air go into your lungs.
Notice your shoulders relaxing.
Focus on how your body feels.
Gently chase away any thoughts that try to invade this space.

Feel that Breath as if it is a warm flame...

(OR - a cool flame if you prefer!)

filling every piece of your body down through your toes.

The first few dozen times are difficult.
Soon you can give yourself ten minutes a day
to bring your mind and body to a peaceful place.

Intention:
Peace.

## 9. Move

*Endorphins, Endorphins, ENDORPHINS!*

*Or, as Elle Woods from Legally Blonde says,*
*"Happy people don't kill their husbands."*

Listen, we don't have to be an exercise guru.
We don't have to be good at anything we do.
Running (mostly) sucks and it will always suck.
But we can: walk, jog, dance, yoga, step, cycle, or throw balls in baskets all the way to contentment.
Moving in some way will force
those good chemicals into circulation.
As with all natural processes,
this takes more than a minute to begin to feel different.
Commit to fifteen minutes, then maybe a half hour.
Self-care through Moving will be fundamental
if we are to move down our Path with our sanity intact.

And remember to keep breathing!

Walk ten minutes if that's all we can do.
Move everyday for a month?
We will feel better.
Physical health will follow if we are on the Journey.
For now, we are Moving for mental health.
If you already are in a little bit of shape, great. Keep moving,
change it up, find something that clears your mind
as well as moves your body.

Everyone, try yoga a few times, if only to understand what it means
to not be perfect and to be okay with that.

Intention:
How can I move to improve my mental health?

# 10. Maintain

*You have cleansed your past, your mind,*
*and you are beginning to cleanse your body.*

This is a *marathon* and we are going to *walk*
deliberately down the Path.
Remember every single day:
it isn't perfection we seek, it's the Journey.
So keep moving forward, keep trying.
Celebrate the moments that you notice improvement.
Did you touch your toes?
Did you not scream at your daughter?
Did you run a mile?
Whatever it is, it's the right thing for right now.
Are there things you want to improve on?
Maybe you did scream at your daughter.
Maybe you snapped at that well-meaning
(but totally annoying) guy in the office.
Maybe you binged Netflix and blew off the day.

That's OKAY! And - that's the point.

You are on the Path now,
and you can commit to doing better tomorrow. And then do it.
Look at the things you want to improve everyday
and don't persecute yourself.
Be kind to yourself, pick reasonable daily goals.
*Today, I will make all of my own meals...*
Develop self empathy.
Keep coming back around to this idea of Maintaining the Path.
This is your habit of self-accountability *without* self-persecution.

Be Proud! This is Your Journey

Intention:
What did I do today that I am proud of? What needs some more practice?

## 11. Practice Self Compassion

*Self improvement doesn't mean self mutilation.*

People don't become their unique version of successful because they did everything perfect all the time. They became that person because the voice in their head didn't tell them they sucked.

She said something more like,
*"Hey, go ahead and try! Nothing ventured, nothing gained."*

Then, if it was a dud of an attempt, she says,
*"It's okay that didn't work out. Here is how we can move forward and try again."*

Sometimes this is easier said than done. Often, we compare our timelines and accomplishments to dozens of other people. We self-mutilate our mental health with varying degrees of self-hatred.

NOPE NOPE NOPE.

Really and truly, who cares what anyone else on the planet thinks? Say you want to learn to paint. You take a class or find a YouTube video and you practice. You suck for a while, and then you paint a flower that you really like! You show people and they are all supportive. Then this guy interjects and says, "I mean, it's alright."

*Stop.* You like your art and that is truly all that matters. Keep painting. Paint not to prove him wrong, paint because you want to paint. Paint more. Paint elaborate flowers. Paint *your* flowers. When you practice self-compassion, inevitably you feel compassion for others. And the world really needs so much more of that.

Intention:
What compassionate words can you say to yourself
in your breathing exercise?

## 12. Help Someone Else

When all else fails—
get outside of your head.

Sometimes we spin circles in our own head.
Even though these little life lessons seem simple,
our brains can really take us on a whirlwind.
When we feel like everyone and everything
is a weight on our shoulders, stop.
Do something lovely for someone else and don't take the credit.
Go visit a nursing home, a soup kitchen, a dog pound.
Do something for someone else,
because spending anymore time in your own head
will just do more damage.
This is an exercise in getting you to see the world
outside the internal miasma.
Refocus that lens on something other than pain.
It is also good to recognize when we feel
persecuted and put upon. It is our own self that is the problem.
That spinning is a form of self-obsession.

*Not to worry! We aren't perfect!*

The solution is to get outside our head and help others.
When this becomes a habit, it is a great outlet.
It can lead to meeting amazing people and communities.
Volunteers are needed in virtually every corner of the world.
We could even just help a friend redecorate their living room.
Or take that special needs cousin to the grocery.
Or help your mother-in-law organize her closet.
Just do something for someone
and get outside of the negative headspace
and into service of others.

Intention:
What can we do to help someone today?

# 13. Gratitude

## This is the Capstone of Happiness

There is nothing more important when going along on this Journey, than a pervasive and consistent sense of Gratitude.

You are bombarded daily with social media, advertising, movies, magazines, and television. All of these things can lead us down the path of envy, comparison, self-loathing, and a general fear of not being good enough.

## The "Less-Than Syndrome"

When we are stuck in a feeling of being less than other people, *gratitude is the prescription.*

No one is as fabulous as they seem.
Some people *are* content, though.

Look at them closely.
They always have a sense of gratitude for their lives.
If you struggle with feeling grateful, start with one thing a day. Maybe a child, a favorite pair of jeans, the local park, your favorite tree, dog, friend, anything that signifies positivity in your life should be rewarded with gratitude.

This takes practice.

Practice daily.

Intention:
What am I grateful for?

# Celebrate The Moment

## 14. Celebrate Differences

It's a big damn WORLD &
Sometimes people think differently.

*Start by rearranging how we respond to new information fundamentally.*

If it is new and different, give it a chance.
When we see something new or learn something new
where does it land in our brain?
Does it land in our amygdala? *(aka. primitive brain)*
Or does it land in our frontal brain?
Do we feel it in our gut?
Or do we respond logically?

If we feel it in our gut, Stop!
Understand this is not a rational reaction to anything.
If we have a visceral response to information,
this is because we have placed this information
in a lower part of our brain.
It is important to recognize that reaction.
If we learn to *differentiate our fear-based reactions from logical thinking* we will truly open up our minds.
Sometimes our opinions are actually wrong,
or unhealthy, or divisive. Sometimes they aren't.
The point is, don't toss away something new because it feels wrong.
Take it out of your amygdala
and have a good look at the information.

Be truly OPEN to learning.

Intention:
What am I facing today that brings me fear?
Why am I reacting this way?

# 15. Become Willing

*Easy for you to say...*

*How do you just become willing?*

Open your mind.
Go back to that place where we cleared off the table.
This is your Journey.
This is your new Path.
When that voice in your head says you *can't*,
you need to immediately tell it you *can*.
This needs to become your new instinct.
Only you can change that voice!

This is a training exercise.
Becoming Willing takes practice
and an attitude that is not so stuck in one's head.
Don't be judgemental of the self or others.
It requires an attitude that is more positive or upbeat!

Intention:
What could I do if I allowed myself to do it?

## 16. Practice Forgiveness

Forgive them; Forgive Yourself.

So much of what makes us unhappy lies in our perception of what *other people* have done wrong, or what *we've* done wrong.

Don't do that! We're on the Path now.
We can Forgive and not live in anger.
Someone told us a long time ago
that it was important for other people to
behave the way we think they should,
and that we need to behave even better than that.

The only thing that comes out of this kind of thinking is self-punishment. Self-punishment serves no purpose.

*Self constructive criticism* is useful. Self-punishment is misery.
It's a form of self-obsession, this need to live in our own suffering.
Forgive yourself, because it is the right and healthy thing to do.

Also – this suffering is Annoying behavior.

In the other direction,
punishing others also leads to misery,
because we have no control over the way others behave.
So how about a little grace?
How about a little sunlight?

Maybe the groovy hippies are a little bit right...

Intention:
Do I have to be *right*? Can I just *be*?

## 17. Clean Out Your Closet

Physically? Like really clean out my closet?

I mean, yeah, you can clean out your closet
if that's all you can handle right now, mentally.
Do something to clean out your space.

But, more importantly,
in order to be on the Journey
and not fall back into old ways that are unhelpful to you,
you need to clean out your *Mental Closet.*

Make sure you are letting go
of all the old behaviors that hold you back.

Some days that means we clean out our Mental Closet.
Other days we are tired
and we might just clean out that drawer in our bathroom.

(Literally)

And that is okay.
Either way we feel better about ourselves afterwards.

Listen, life on a path requires
maintenance.

Intention:
What can I do today to clean my Path?

## 18. Invite Others In

*You just cleaned out your closet right?*

If we are on a Path
we understand that life is change.
We are constantly working towards a better self,
not *perfectly* working towards a better self, but *constantly*.
We understand that we've done some things here and there
that we are not proud of.

Don't hide those things.
I mean, don't go out and tell everybody all of the terrible things
you've done. That's just annoying.

But make yourself vulnerable.
Allow close, trusted friends to know you truly.
And then, allow some other friends to know you a little better.

You'd be surprised how that helps other people as well as yourself.
On the Path, when we practice grace,
we want other people to benefit from our Journey.

Intention:
Can I help someone else today
by making myself a little vulnerable?

## 19. Love Without Expectation

Stop. Keeping. Score.

Friendship, family, love, work, etc.
These things do not have a scoreboard.

When we want true happiness,
we must let go of Expectations.

If we do something, make sure our intentions
are for the sake of doing that thing.
Don't do something to make someone owe us.
If we give, we must give freely without Expectation.

This will relieve an incredible amount of stress in our soul.
On the Path we are not the grand master or scorekeeper.
So don't act like one.

If you are saying,
"but surely you don't mean all the time, money,
labor, etc that I give".
This means anything you give.
When you give, just give.
Can you imagine how much less stress
you would have in your life
if you truly didn't keep score?

Intention:
Do I give without expecting anything in return?
Can I actually see the world that way?

# 20. Believe In Yourself

Cue the Disney Princess Music—

But seriously...
Think hard about this moment.
If you allow the external world to define you,
you will never move forward.

If you allow that Bitch in Your Head to be your guide...
you will be listening to the *wrong you.*

Grab hold of that princess you once believed in.
Nobody needs to know what your inner voice looks like or says.
Maybe it's not a Disney princess,
but more of the Tomb Raider type.
Who cares!

Just find the voice that once told you that you were awesome!
And *sing and scream and celebrate* with that voice.

If you don't remember a Disney princess
or a kick ass super hero, good news!
We have an abundance of characters to choose from today.
Or, you can make one up.

Either way, choose a better voice to listen to.
And then believe in that voice.

Intention:
Who or what do I want to be my spirit guide today?

# 21. Believe In Balance

This can be done in tiny little ways.

As with all things,
when you think about Change and Balance
it may seem overwhelming.

Good News!

You are on this Path that allows you to do *little* things
so that, eventually, you can do *kick ass* things.
Maybe... just start with a little Balance.
Maybe you drink a glass of wine *(or 5...)*
when you get home from work.
Maybe you don't do the yoga, or you don't go on the walk.
Maybe you've started something 15 times.
Maybe you don't cut yourself any slack, so, eventually you quit.
Balance means *allowing* yourself to *fail*.
If you start something and give up, you can always try again.
There is no rule about Balance in your life;
just the fact that we need to find a way to Balance the good and the bad, the fun and the mundane, and the tough with the relaxing.
Who doesn't love a good Netflix binge?
But, you can't do that every day.

It's really not healthy.

Working towards Balance is about a gentle change.
Maybe take a night to write a poem.
Do that yoga. Take a walk. Write a letter.
Do something to Balance out whatever you do too much of.
Because that is being kind to yourself.
Then, make a habit of being kind to yourself.

Intention:
Do I need to Balance something in my life?

## 22. Keep On Track By Keeping Track

Sounds like work.

*It can't all be simple.*

But really - it isn't complicated!

Being your best you is good for you,
good for your family,
good for everyone you come in contact with.

In order to hold yourself accountable to something,
you must keep track of it.

Pick something that you have placed in your Path
and hold yourself responsible for it.
In other words, keep track of whether or not
you're achieving your goals.

Make it simple at first,
so that you don't fall back into self-abuse.

Find a journal that you can use to to keep track of your goals
and in a year you can look back and see how far you've come.

If it's doing yoga once a week,
this is an a *huge accomplishment*
if you haven't done something like this before.
Don't discount any achievement - even if you see it as small.

Intention:
What should I start keeping track of?

# 23. Allow For Failure

Some days – nothing goes as planned.

There will be other days. There will be better days.
If you are on the Path to Becoming,
then you understand perfection is not the goal.

Some days you intend to do 1001 things,
and you don't even get 1 done.
Some days you forget to hit the
*"I am a nice person"* reset button on the way out the door,
and it all comes out s i d e w a y s.

Tomorrow, you get to *still be* on the Path.
Walking the Journey requires patience.
Remember that self-abuse is ultimately self-obsession.
Don't waste that mental obsession
on something as ugly as self-hatred.

Commit to giving yourself the day.
Take the mulligan.
But, here is the ticket:
Commit to getting up tomorrow,
and staying on the Path.

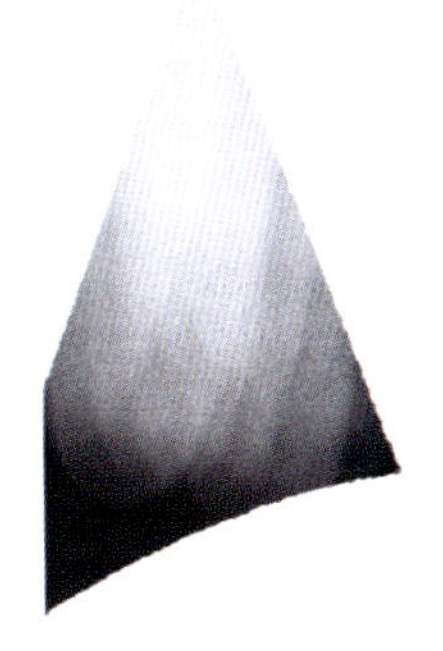

Intention:
Am I too hard on myself?

## 24. You Do Not Bear It All

*You really don't control everything— so it's not all yours to bear*

You thought you had to control the outcome of that 5th grader's soccer game, or the response of the ad agency to your portfolio, or that woman's response to your new haircut.

Sooooo much freedom comes when you realize you don't have to do that!

You don't need to control anything outside of your own responses. Place those worries aside. Put them in a worry box! Meditate and clear your mind.

Meditation works and there is great science behind it.

Maybe, investigate a spiritual practice. Find a community that builds you up, and gobbles up all that negativity for you. Find God, or, a Goddess if that works for you. If we haven't mentioned this before, all rules are out the window when you are on the Path. Investigate what you really believe, or even what you *want* to believe, and then dive deep.

This is where you find out that you are not alone. Whether it be a community of witches, a Christian church, a yoga studio, a Buddhist temple, an intellectual community that focuses on well- being, a pagan circle, a twelve step program, a synagogue, a counseling group, or whatever--whatever community you find, allow it to take some of the weight of the world off of your shoulders.

Intention:
Can I place my worries in something outside myself?

## 25. Go Through Pain

No – this is Not a Sports Ad.

This doesn't mean "work through the Pain, baby!"

It means live through the Pain, and make sure you don't stay there.
Think of how you see yourself, how you describe yourself.
Is your go-to self definition steeped in some kind of trauma?
It is time to move through that.

Get a counselor, self-help group, or treatment, and stop letting this aspect of your life define you. Go through the Pain.

Don't choose to suffer forever. This goes for little daily life choices as well. Does everything happen *to* you? Are you constantly being put upon? Do you feel like no one understands?

Maybe you need a counselor. Maybe you just need to change your perspective. You are on the Path now, and the Path doesn't suffer Debbie Downers.

This being said, you are absolutely allowed to have bad days. You are absolutely allowed to have pain. You are absolutely allowed to fail. Just don't stay there. It really is that simple. The only person making you stay in that shit is you.

Get back on the Path, forgive yourself,
forgive them, and move through the Pain.

Intention:
Do I Suffer?

## 26. Celebrate The Moment

Every. Damn. Thing.

Celebrate the things big and small.
Everyday.

Find one thing in the midst of the chaos that makes you smile. Even if you have to use YouTube to find that thing. Make a habit of finding something to smile about, something to get excited about.

Not just the lip-service kind of excitment, but the 'holy cow life is amazing' kind of bliss. No one can tell you where to find this.

Some people may find it in a meaningful conversation. Other people find it through their family or by experiencing new things.

This habit of Celebration, more than anything else,
can make life more bearable. Practicing Celebration only brings more joy, contentment, and appreciation to every day.

Then, you won't mind forgiving.

You don't have to live in suffering.
You can become willing,
and that leads to a life worth living.

Intention:
What can I truly Celebrate today?

# Understand Grace

# 27. Change Is Necessary

*It doesn't have to be painful.*

*EMBRACE IT.*

Your children Grow.
Friends Change.
Pets get old.
You age.

Life happens.
We move on.

Sometimes we resist the inevitable.

But, with every Change,
the space left behind allows for Growth.
Growth is how we live our best lives.

So, embrace Change.
It's the one thing in life that is certain.
It is the only way to Grow.

When the Tides of Change hit your door,
do what you need to do to Adjust emotionally.
Then, move forward and Grow.

Don't stay behind.

Intention:
What change am I resisting?

# 28. Surrender

This doesn't mean — BE A LOSER.

Understand that this is a win.
This is the plea to stop fighting healthy things,
To stop fighting anything out of your comfort zone,
To stop fighting solutions.

Get comfortable with the idea that
*you don't know everything*,
and that it's *okay*.
This, in fact, is the only way we learn.
Surrender to the idea that you are on the Journey,
and you are here to learn.
You cannot move forward until you surrender old ideas.
There is so much to see out there
if you can get out of your own way.

Intention:
Think of something that is out of your comfort zone.
Can you change how you see that thing?

## 29. Nurture Yourself

Right, but how?

Nurturing Yourself isn't just about going to the spa or getting a back rub. I mean, those things are all great and can be part of Nurturing yourself--but that's not all of it.

You need to develop a habit of checking in with Yourself. You are the only person responsible for your own well-being. It is important to have regular check-ins with your Mind, your Body, and your Spirit.

Nurturing Yourself means checking in with Yourself, and then doing what needs to be done. If you are tired, that's easy.

Sleep ~ Always remember how important Sleep is.

If you are anxious, there is probably a reason why. You can talk it through with a counselor or a friend. Maybe you need to take a walk or run, and get those endorphins going. Sometimes, we are just chemically imbalanced. Or sometimes you need to pamper yourself with a day of relaxation. Or meditation. Or a backrub.

Okay – Sometimes you just need a day at the Spa.

The point is, Nurturing Yourself needs to become a habit.

Intention:
How can I Nurture my Mind, Body, and Spirit today?

## 30. See The Bigger Picture

Perspective is a game changer.

If we feel we are holding the world on our shoulders,
it is time to take that globe off our back,
and set it down in front of us.

Taking a look at our *small part* in this great wide world
can make us see how infinitesimal our concerns often are.

Usually, the thing that makes us angry, *is us.*
Even when we are being attacked,
we have the capacity to control our reaction to it.

We can always change how we see things.
The Journey allows for frequent paradigm shifts.
This is what it means to go through life.

Even in the face of terrible moments,
we know that we will make it to the other side.

You may be better for the experience, despite the pain.
This kind of perspective is what the Path is all about.

Intention:
Do I recognize when I blow things out of proportion?

## 31. Speak Your Truth

It will help You.
It will help them.

This isn't preaching. This is sharing.
This is allowing yourself the freedom to tell your story.
Other people feel the same way that you do,
or have been through a similar experience.

This is how we heal.
This is how we bring people together.
This is true bonding.

When you are able to speak your truth,
people will know you are sincere.
This is how you help them.
This is how you help yourself.

Everyone responds to that kind of vulnerability and honesty.
It shines through the bullshit.

Intention:
What is your Truth today?
How can you work towards more serenity?

# 32. Meet People Where They Are

But people can be so annoying...

This doesn't say look down on people.
It says meet people where they are.
Try to understand where they are coming from.
This is frequently difficult when we disagree with someone.
That is when it is most important to stop, breathe,
and try to walk in their shoes.

This is what it means to be empathetic.
This is also a recipe to reduce stress in your life.
All of those people who annoy you,
can now be met with a little more compassion,
and a lot less frustration.

Intention:
What do I learn from the People in my life?

## 33. You Can't Please Everyone

BUT ~ You can die trying!

Literally.
People Pleasing leads to frustration and anxiety.
This state of being leads to immunosuppression.
Prolonged immunosuppression can cause cancer.
You can literally die trying to please people.
The best way to fundamentally please the people in your life,
is to take care of yourself.

Once you have taken care of yourself,
you develop the confidence you need
to be of service to the people around you.

Sometimes that takes a little bit of time.
So, go ahead and do what you need to do
to make yourself healthy.

Intention:
Do I spin my wheels trying to please others?

## 34. Live In The Moment

*"The here and now is all we have, and if we play it right it's all we'll need." ~ Ann Richards*

There are a couple tenents to this.

First, don't dwell on the Past. Don't live in a moment that brought you pain. Don't ruminate endlessly about what you could have done different.

You have the ability to deal with it!

Get a counselor. Talk to a friend or family member. Get through it. Don't live there. You are missing out on making new Memories while you roll around in all that gooey, painful Past.

Another tenent is the Future.

Ohhh ~ the ANXIETY!

JUST STOP. The future will happen and you can plan for it... however, you cannot control it.

Besides, you are on a Journey now; you can handle it.

Whatever it is...

That "Future Anxiety" is just another manifestation of that Bitch in your head and she still isn't welcome here.

Intention:
What keeps my mind from staying present?

## 35. Nourish Yourself

*Let's start with the fact that your body is beautiful,*
*and no matter what, you must always know that this is true.*

Food is part of the chemical processes in our body.
This affects moods, energy, and yes, self-esteem.

We are committed to Journeying now;
eating has to be a part of it.
We will not be perfect.

Instead of obsessing
about how we fail or win at food,
we should educate ourselves about it.

We aren't talking about the latest fad diet or food trend.
Investigate the consequences of industrial farming,
and the farm to table movement.

When we understand how food is produced
we can make more conscientious decisions
about what we use to fuel our body,
and how that affects our mental health.

Eventually, this will change our relationship with food.
We will never be perfect on this Path,
but the seeds we plant will grow.

Intention:
Do I understand how food is related to how I feel?

# 36. Dance

In the rain! With socks on!

*No; just kidding.*
*Don't do the sock thing.*

Unless that's your idea of being wild, then,
of course, by all means, Dance with soggy socks on.
The point is — move with joyful purpose.

You know that feeling when you're spinning around? No, not the feeling that you're going to barf. The one where your heart feels like it's going to burst with happiness. That is what you want to channel. Channel *joy*.

Dance down the hallway. Choose to feel that elation, and carry it into your day. Don't worry about other peoples' happiness.

This kind of happy is infectious.

Try the revolutionary idea of sharing that bursting energy (or anxiety) in a positive light. When someone else wants to hate your dance, it's your decision to let them in your head.

Dance harder!

... and tell them to $!@# off!

Intention:
Can you be ecstatic without worrying what anyone thinks?

## 37. Move Your Mind

Just as you must stretch your body,
You must stretch your mind.

Watch a documentary about food,
religions in the world,
the oceans, or art.

Read or listen to a book.
Investigate educational programs that interest you
even if you aren't planning on going back to school.

Don't just fall into an internet rabbit hole.
Spend some time learning.
And if you do enter
an opinionated, internet rabbit hole
check your resources.
Especially, if you agree with the information.
Expand your mind; don't live in your echo chamber.

Intention:
If I could learn about anything, what would it be?

## 38. Show The World Happiness

Don't be afraid to celebrate your victories.

There is truth to "you get what you give."
If you want everyone else to have a better attitude,
the best place to start is with yourself.

This doesn't mean don't stand up for yourself,
or be a docile wall flower.

Never!

This means empower yourself with an internal flame of happiness. This is actually a superpower. If you hone your ability to be positive, you will build emotional Teflon armor. Bullshit doesn't stick to you.

And instead of coating yourself in a blanket of misery, fear and self-induced suffering, you get to be happy!

Done well, this is the greatest gift. With a little practice, you would be amazed at how everyone around you will begin to act differently.

By putting this out to the world, you create protection against misery. It boosts your confidence and allows you to face challenges head on without all that distrust.

Intention:
Can I pause my negativity and trust that a happy attitude will create a better world?

# 39. Understand Grace

*"To be a light to others you will need a good dose of the spiritual life. Because as my mother used to say, if you are in a good place, then you can help others; but if you're not well, then go look for somebody who is in a good place who can help you." ~ Rigoberta Menchu*

Cultivating empathy, happiness,
self-love, and surrender
allows space for miracles.

Grace is another superpower
that you can show people.
Grace can enter your total being
and make you feel like the world is worth it.

When you have compassion for yourself and others,
you are able to access this empowering concept,
and let the endorphin-filled feeling wash over you.

Understand that these ways of being
are actually empowering.
These ways of being allow you to find Grace.

It can be as versatile as the word F*ck.
You can show Grace, be filled with Grace,
say Grace, give Grace,
and on and on.

It is Becoming. It is Knowing. It is the Path.
Be open to understanding Grace.

Intention:
Am I resisting happiness? Why? Can I be open to Grace?

# Do Unto Others

## 40. Check Yourself

Your butt looks great — DO NOT worry about that!

All these concepts and goals are not an immediate thing.
Committing to a Journey is completely fluid.
Like a river, or a fondue pot, or sexuality.

It flows in different ways.
We try. We fail. We try again.

In the trying, we Become. All of this begins with the simple idea that we need to Check ourselves.
We need to weed out what makes us unhappy, and the primary thing that makes us unhappy — is us.
Focus on the things we need to change within our own wheelhouse.

As with everything on our Journey, this is actually empowering.
When we focus inwardly, we can affect real change in our lives.
When we look at others and try to change, compare, or affect them, the only result is stress.

So, look at your own faults.

We all have them.

Put all your energy there and live by example.

Intention:
Do I really see myself —
both the good and the "needs work" parts?

## 41. See The Good

Know you are extraordinary!

We have chastised the voice in your head,
but we haven't changed the message to something new.
You don't know where this Path will lead,
and that is exciting.

Inside, you have all these hopes and dreams.
Why not greet the day like you already know
you are headed towards them?
Not with arrogance, but with (yes, again) joy.
Then, it doesn't take anything from you to
treat everyone else the same way.
With confidence in your own extraordinary self,
you can support others in their dreams and hopes.
This will reflect back on you and increase your confidence,
making you even more extraordinary.

Too much? Never-

No one is saying wake up every day
and completely lie about how you are feeling
in the effort to be positive.
That is unrealistic and possibly unbalanced.

The point is to start to replace the negative head space
with an overzealous positive one.
What comes out of that will not be extreme.
It's time to balance the scales of negative thinking
with some extreme positivity.

Intention:
Do I value the dreams and beauty of myself and others?

## 42. Find The Magic

Calm down, this really isn't hokey.

*Not entirely, anyway!*

Okay, so, when you really start to embrace the concept that you are on a Journey and the Path is the goal, you become willing to change. Willingness leads to openness. Openness leads to the ability to see things with child-like eyes.
This allows you to look at the world differently. Not trolls and fairies and vampires, but how the world really is amazing. How we literally don't know shit about most of it, and that is perfectly okay.

That is the magic. We get to spend the rest of our lives learning about whatever we want. And because it's your own damn Path, it can include deep ocean creatures, existentialism, the breeding cycle of peacocks, mountain ranges of the world, fractals, romantic literature, or actual witchcraft.

No one holds power over your Path except you.
You get to completely define what is important to you.
You get to find what magic means to you.

Intention:
What strikes me as magical?

## 43. Let Go Of Those Flaws

*"I allow myself to fail. I allow myself to break. I'm not afraid of my flaws." ~ Lady GaGa*

We love to hang on to bad habits. Gossiping, stirring the pot, hate mongering, drinking (or whatever), bingeing (on anything), shopping, being a know-it-all, lust, gluttony, greed, sloth, and any number of destructive habits are really just bad coping mechanisms.

We get a mini (or major) endorphin rush from these things. That positive reinforcement has taught us that it is okay to do these things to make ourselves feel better. That is why they are hard to let go of. That's okay!

We aren't perfect, and we may fail. Become willing to change and try to address one or two of them at a time.

You are freaking human, and you aren't supposed to be perfect. Don't take that attitude. The all-or-nothing attitude leads to failure.

(Except maybe addiction. If you need help with something that is an addiction, get help for that. This is a priority. Stop right here and call for help. Just do it. No one ever said, "Gosh I wish I would have stayed mired in the hell of my addiction." The sooner you take care of that, the quicker you can get in touch with the Journey to awesomeness.)

Change requires a little commitment and willingness from you. The Journey is constantly changing. You will do what? Try, fail, try again. The only important part in that series is try again. The Law Of Averages says some of those good habits will stick over time.

Intention:
What do I need to change first?

# 44. Let It Be

*Repeat the mantra,*
*'I would rather be content than right.'*

This is probably one of the hardest things to do
because people are so freaking stupid
and they should all think exactly like me...right?

But, if we slow down and get out of our lower brain,
we can elevate to a place of logic.
Not 'why don't they see it my way',
but 'why do they feel the way they do?'.

This kind of thinking leads to understanding
or at the very least diffuses anger.
When you can't bring it to the frontal brain, walk away.
Give yourself time to let your primitive brain calm down.
Even if you are fundamentally correct,
no one ever hears a counterpoint through seething anger.

If you can bring an argument to a discussion level
and hear what the other person is saying,
you can learn so much more about
why there has to be discussion in the first place.

This also begs the point that
you need to be able to articulate
why you feel the way you do.
If you don't have enough information to do that,
then you probably really need to hear
what the other person has to say.
Sometimes we are wrong.

Intention:
Can I listen to someone who thinks differently than me,
and let it be?

## 45. Be An Example

a good one?

Yes, a good one. But that doesn't mean you have to be a perfect angel who never questions the rules.

It does, however, mean you should develop
standards and see the world globally.
When you are an employee,
or a parent, or part of some group,
no one cares what you say.
It's what you *do* that means something.

People can talk all day saying all the right things,
but unless you walk the walk, it's meaningless.
Parents can tell their kids to be kind,
but unless they example how to do that,
the child won't really know.

An employee can say they worked hard
but let someone else do all their work.
You can tell the group you are fine,
but they will see only your actions.

You don't have to be perfect, but you do have to be aware.
Being aware requires that you see your world
from more than just a place of '*poor me and my circumstance.*'

It requires you to look at everyone else involved in the situation.
It requires action and empathy. Now that you are on the Path and doing all of the things, this will be a lot easier!

Intention:
Am I the person I say I am?

## 46. Not Everyone Is On Your Path

Am I even on the path?

We start to embrace a little joy.
We start to investigate the healthy things.
We start to live with a little intention.

Then some asshole says something
that rips your soul out of your chest
and you are reaching for the desk ruler
to craft a shiv and end the bastard where they stand.
We are human. Maybe don't kill them.

But also, do not let them rent space in your head.
This is where you have control.
Letting this loser hang out in your brain,
for more than the required 30 seconds of conflict, is all on you.
That primadonna is an asshole.
Why would you give them that kind of luxury
to stay in your mind?

Instead, back up and understand something.
One, you may not have understood their intent.
Really. We aren't perfect.
(And some of us always think that people are saying negative things about us.)
Or two, they are clearly not well, or content, or adjusted.
They have to live with themselves every second, every damn day.

That is your consolation. Yes, you are on the Path.
You get to get better every day!

Intention:
Do I let people's behavior toward me control how I see myself?

## 47. Try New Things

*Just try the thing.*

Let go of the fear of things
that are different than you.

If something, a place, a topic, a style of music gives you almost
a physical negative reaction, that is fear.

Take a closer look at that. Music is a simple one. If you have a
volatile reaction to a certain type of music, it is likely fear based
and deep seated in something you were taught.

Say you were taught that a style of music objectifies women or
makes them look bad. Or perhaps that you were taught that likeing
another style of music makes you "less-than".

But have you ever listened to the styles you a bias against?

We were all taught stupid shit. It is really not worth living in fear
of those things that are different than you, especially when they can
bring you as much joy as music can.

Rise above!
And try the thing that you were taught was wrong.

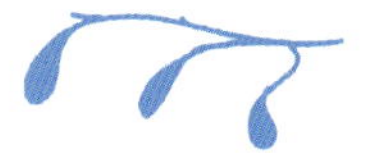

Intention:
What thing do I react to negatively without logic?

## 48. See Through A Different Lens

the world can really be amazing!

This cannot be clear enough.
This is a choice.
We can stay in a negative space
or move into a world where we choose
to see the good.

Sometimes you will feel
that this is next to impossible.
Take that breath.
Put your new glasses on
and see whatever corner of the world
that brings you a positive vibe.
Yes, vibe.

(Because this is not a defined social science there aren't precise words to describe things like vibes, but you know what it means.)

Access those feelings by focusing
on something positive
in the world.

Even a painting in the corner
of the room can be transformative,
if you give it a chance.

Recite a poem or a mantra or a prayer
and give all the negativity away.
Choose to see the world as a beautiful space.

Intention:
What can I focus on to put my
head in a positive place?

# 49. Look At Yourself Clearly

Wipe the grit off the glass.

No one can do this perfectly.
It is a daily mental exercise.
Did someone react to you unexpectedly?
That may be on them, yes.
But see if you can look at your part in that moment.
Did you come off in a harsh way that you were unaware of?
Is this person really sensitive and you are unaware of that?
Do you apologize too much?
Do you blame others all the time?
Do you try to hide your guilt?
(It never works, by the way.)

Guess what?
This is a Journey and you are not perfect,
so lay off yourself.
Denial, shame, and hiding prevent you
from actually becoming the kick ass,
self-realized human that you are.

So look at it and try to do better next time.
As time moves on you will be amazed
at how much more easily you can breathe.

Intention:
What is something that I don't like to see in
myself? Can I admit it and try a little harder?

## 50. Look For The Spark In You

This is that dig deep kind of thing.

It is so important to validate the thing inside of you that gives life meaning. The spirit, the soul, the collaboration of hormones that make life feel important, the collective consciousness, the genetic connection, or maybe even just the plain old senses. Whatever it is that you need to do to allow yourself to connect with this essential part of who you are, start looking at that. For ease of definition here, let's call it spirit or spiritual sense of self.

We are on a path of self-improvement that is about the mind-body-spirit connection. We build walls against this connection. Sometimes we were taught a punishing God. That has zero to do with this. Sometimes, we are atheists and cannot abide discussions of God. Again, zero to do with this. The scientific community can describe hormones and chemicals that elevate our moods or create disfunction. We cannot, however, explain why a person with a spiritual sense of self seems to do better emotionally in life. Furthermore, if you are of the godly type, no one can prove arguments in that direction either. We used to live in caves and grunt at each other. But, here's the deal. Who the @#$% cares? As long as you look inward and find what ever *it* is.

If you embrace some sort of spiritual sense of self, you will be more content. It could be straight up meditation. You don't need to believe in God to do that. Or it could be prayer and church. Or it could be rituals with crystals and tarot. There are as many religions, spiritual practices and meditative exercises as there are people on this planet. It is nobody's business what you do to hone that spark in you. This is a really important part of this journey, so start digging.

Intention:
How do we see ourselves spiritually? Can we grow a spiritual or meditative sense of self?

# 51. See The Spark In Everyone

*"Luminous beings are we... not this crude matter."*
*~ Yoda, from the Empire Strikes Back.*

Not only can we look at our spiritual sense of self,
but we can look for it in others.
This is easy with some people if you like and identify with them.
Understanding that we all are somewhere
in the process of Becoming,
helps us to be more compassionate,
more forgiving and actually mean it.

We want to learn how to see others
more compassionately, more often.
When you see that person who
crawls right down your craw,
and brings out the ugly self,
pause.

Identify one thing that you think
this person is struggling with.
Identify one thing that they do well.
Identify one annoying thing they do, that you also do.

One of these things is the calming ticket.
You don't have to love them with all your soul.
You only need to look into their soul.
It is really hard to hate someone
if you actually take the time to see them.

Intention:
Can I see the good in people today?

## 52. Do Unto Others

*This is the basis of everything spiritually and mentally healthy.*

If only we could support, love,
care for, raise up, and bond with others
the way we would like to be treated,
the world would be amazing.

It is so impressive how many of us think
we are being fair,
but don't actually see those around us.
This "seeing others" removes
so much stress in our lives.

We suddenly understand
that no one is really thinking about us.
Everyone is busy trying to get through the day.
If we let go of worrying about what others are doing or thinking
and only focus on doing the right thing in our own actions,
we become amazingly calm.

You don't have to do these things
because it is moral high ground,
or you are going to hell if you don't.
You do these things
because it is just so much less stressful
to worry about everyone else's behavior
than it is to focus on our own.
And by having the singular focus
of your own behavior,
you can really become the person you want to be.

Intention:
Can I stop focusing on what others are doing,
and focus on my own Journey?

# Laugh And The World Laughs With You

## 53. Drop It

like it's hot.
(Really, could anything else follow that?)

It is really hard to focus
on mental health
when we are juggling
and fighting
and struggling and trying. Stop.

This is so hard to wrap
your head around,
but in order to become
the kick ass warrior
that is inside of you,
it is important to stop the struggle.

If you want to break through
to a better place
you have to submit
to the things that will help
rather than hinder you.

Sometimes our brains tell us
we don't have to do "the things"
that will move us to a better place.
Stop fighting. Do all of the things.

Now, you can become the true you.
Not a fighter, but an empowered warrior.

Intention:
Can I stop focusing on what others are doing and focus on my own Journey?

## 54. Forget About It

But it REALLY Pissed me off!

*2001 called. They want their resentment back.*

For that matter,
last week wants all their vinegar back too.

Think hard. Why did this situation piss you off?
If you don't have a part in the situation,
it tends not to stick to your rib cage and fester in your gut.
When someone does something horrid and you don't have (at the very least) ego invested in it, they don't burn a lasting mark on you.

For instance, this guy at work discounts you and talks over you. So what? He's an asshole. But for some reason he is really latching on to your frontal lobe and you can't stop thinking about him.

Your ego is hurt because he doesn't recognize you for your talents.
Is he an asshole? Of course, he is.

Does he deserve all that frontal lobe attention?

Ummm, he has already been an asshole. Why are you devoting another minute to it? Now, no one is good at this completely. We get better with practice. We focus on the fact that it is only our egos that make us want to force this guy to see our value.

We sacrifice our happiness on resentment.

Intention:
Who am I raging against in my life? Why?
What purpose does it serve?

# 55. Embrace It

*If it is going to help you in your life,*
*you should love it.*

That sounds so simple, right?
But we build walls and prejudices
against things that would help us.

We think of these walls as principles
or some kind of moral code or values.
We may be afraid of being weird or different than our peers.
We belittle things even though we think we are open minded.
We fight admitting a simple truth.

If something would help us become a better person,
why in the name of all that is holy or unholy
would you not embrace it?

What is stopping you other than you?

You are on the damn Path now!

Who cares what all those rules
in your head have been telling you.
Do the things to make you feel,
think, and be a better person.
The absolute promise is that you will be happier,
and you will inherently start to really kick some ass.

Intention:
What do you fight against that you know deep down
would be a healthy choice?

## 56. Think On It

I mean, don't lose your marbles or anything.

Go back over the Journey so far.
Look at all the things, good and bad,
and develop a little clarity on where you are today.
A journal can help. Review the choices,
the situations, the people.
Understand *your part* in sticky situations.
Look at how awesome you are at some other things.

If you have trouble identifying those things,
get a counselor. Develop self-knowledge.
Work to really see who you are and why.
Do this without living in miserable self-judgement.

You are on the Path!
You can move down this road to the next junction
without staying in mistakes.
The mistakes are just that: learning tools.
Time to understand that you are a collection
of beautiful and not so beautiful moments.

:)

Your next move is the most important one.

Intention:
What can you do today to take stock of your life?

# 57. Give It Up

For the Path and the Journey!! (Roar of the Crowd)

Actually, you should practice giving up things.

Not to be completely austere,
but to learn how to create healthy habits and develop grit.
You get better at things the more you practice them.
Quitting unhealthy habits and behaviors
requires the same kind of practice.
So, you want to quit drinking wine or smoking?
Quit. You fail, try again.
You fail.
You try again.
Eventually you find something that helps you quit again.
Maybe you join a group.
Maybe you get help through a treatment center.
Maybe you get counseling.
Whatever the thing is that is keeping you unhealthy,
learn how to get it out of your life!

No one is saying this is easy.

If they are, they are an lying,
and we don't care what anyone else says anyway.
The question is when you are looking at your life
and being honest with yourself,
these things do not serve you in the long run,
so why do we grasp on to them?

Intention:
What things do I need to eliminate from my life to be happy and healthy in the long run?

# 58. See How Others Do It

## Do What Exactly?

Like, everything and anything.
What are others doing that amazes you or draws you to them?
Who embodies characteristics you value?
How exactly do they do that?
Figure that out. Look at real life examples around you.
Make sure when you do this, however, you check your value system and see that they are healthy. Sometimes healthy options seem bland and boring and drab.

But that is not this Journey--
the Journey is whatever you make it.

Find people who have a zest for life
but aren't themselves disasters.
If you don't have exposure to people like that,
seek them out through any number of hobby groups,
spiritual groups, or intellectual pursuits.
Healthy people are happier over time.
Neil Young may have sung "it's better to burn out than to fade away", but he never struggled with heroin and he is still alive and still kicking ass in a number of categories.
Now, Neil Young may not be the best example of a mentor for you but there are likely musicians out there that would say differently.
For us, maybe it's someone like a person at work, a cousin, a person at yoga or church or an author.
If you can't find someone, write down the attributes you value and do a deep dive on the internet.
Turn your ideas upside down
and see how being healthy is revolutionary.

Intention:
Who do I admire?

## 59. Give It Up Again

*Did you think we forgot you quit something?*

Angela Duckworth wrote a book called *Grit*
based on years of research she did
on how perseverance wins over talent.
She actually developed a formula for this.
It's great stuff because it teaches the idea
that you can *learn* this skill.
There has been a lot of research on how to develop
things like perseverance and will-power.
The short story is if you try something
and it doesn't work the first time, try it again.
The other short story is if you have an addiction,

*get help.*

There are plenty of bad habits that require attention.
All of them land somewhere on a spectrum.
Keep quitting until quitting becomes the habit.

Keep trying to better yourself
until self-improvement
becomes the norm.

Intention:
Do I really want to be healthy?

# 60. Let Others See You

WARTS AND ALL.

This is about transparency.
This is about taking off the mask.
Getting your hair done,
dressing daily for *yourself*—
*whatever* you do to feel like your best you, simply shows
that you care enough about yourself to
invest in taking care of yourself.
Don't deny yourself the self-respect of self-care.
These are important rituals that allow you to validate you.

That is not to be confused with attempts to hide who you are.
Sometimes we show only a mask.
Sometimes we hide more than just our face;
we hide any kind of real self from the world.
We are afraid for the world to see who we want to be.
Why are you afraid to be transparently you?

You are walking down a path of self-realization.
Who you want to be
and what you want to look like
are entirely up to you.
There is no need to present yourself as anything
other than 100 percent the person you want to be.
This goes for how you present your internal self.
Authenticity shines through.
Plastic attitudes and plastic presentations
only eat away at you over time.
You are better than that. Be you!

Intention:
Is there a me inside I am afraid to let out?

## 61. Find What You Love

Can I say - Chocolate?

You may,
but that may not be quite as helpful.

This doesn't have to happen tomorrow.
It doesn't have to happen once.
It can be one great fabulous thing after another.
Remember this is a Journey.

The important thing
is that you love yourself enough
to allow yourself to go after your passion.

Maybe it's a hobby, a career,
or an obsession with science fiction.
Maybe it's a crystal collection;
Maybe it is all of those things.

Allow yourself the luxury
of exploring your passions and dreams.
This lights an internal flame
and creates contentment.
That is why this is important.
It is the foundation of the Path.

Passion

Intention:
What is something I have always wanted to do or start?

# 62. Don't Take Yourself So Seriously

Nobody cares, Karen.

Disclaimer: Actual women named Karen weren't used in the making of this joke.

If you find that you are often the one
who is more upset than everyone else,
that may be an indication of self-obsession.
We need to take ourselves less seriously.
In this world of 24-hour-news cycles,
we need to learn to take The World less seriously, too.

That isn't to say you should drop
the important causes in your life; it is a plea for perspective.
At the end of the day we're playing the long game.
You aren't going to make changes over night
and your world isn't falling apart over night.

Breathe

Start with Gratitude;
really learn to enjoy your quirks.
You are learning who you are more deeply.
All the beautiful imperfections can be hilarious!
Your ability to laugh at yourself shields you
from being truly hurt by others.
You have silenced that Bitch in your head;
you won't internalize the judgement of others.
You also won't see others as judging you when they are not.
You will begin to understand that only you
have the ability to hurt you.

Lighten up – & You become Lighter.

Intention:
Can I shrug it off or is everything a great offense?

## 63. Practice Delight

Afternoon Delight?

Hey, have at it!
Listen, it took years to make us sad,
malcontented or miserable.

It will take practice to make us happy.
When you face the day, take a minute
to quiet your mind and find peace.

Then, consciously move forward
with the intention of being happy.
No one is going to do this for you.
You have to make a conscious choice.

Sometimes we fight the ideas of things that are good for us.
Sometimes our toxic pasts will make us resist happiness.

Think for a second about how crazy that is.
Contentment is a state of mind. You have cleared off the table and you are moving forward. Do it. Be happy.

:)

Intention:
Do I resist practicing happiness? Why?

## 64. Notice Others

*This is the classic,*
*"it's not all about you".*

We all struggle with this
to varying degrees.

Taking a minute to really notice
and celebrate others helps remind us to stay grounded.
Give compliments freely
without expecting any back.

This is so empowering
because it takes the comparison game out.
Remember most people are just trying
to make it through their day.

If we get outside our own heads
and spread the love by complimenting,
noticing, and sharing with those around us,
we aren't focusing on what we think others
should be doing for us.

Intention:
Can I engage people around me without expectation?

## 65. Laugh And The World Laughs With You

*You are allowed to have bad days.*

Generally speaking, with practice,
this attitude toward life makes bad days more bearable
and they come less often.

When they (whomever they are)
come after you and you laugh at them,
it is the most disarming moment.
It puts the power back in your hands.

They can't chip away at your dignity
because you are laughing at the situation,
and clearly won't be bothered
with their Negative Nancy ways.

Now, maybe, don't laugh at work
every time there is a crisis, right?
Understand how brightening
the way we respond empowers us to be able to handle it.

We aren't all wrapped up
in the drama and negative chemical responses,
so we can move more efficiently
into handling whatever it is.
Laughter, truly, is the best medicine.

Intention:
Do I know how to see the light side of situations?
Or do I fall quickly into worry?

# If You Knew Everything You Would Be God

## 66. Picture a Body of Water

Is this a meditation?

Take a deep breath and quiet your mind.
Start with three minutes a day.
The great news is your breathing
is always with you,
so you can do this anywhere or anytime.

Focus on your breathing and picture water.
Imagine floating in or simply watching the water—
whatever puts you in the right mindset.

Here is the thing:
You cannot do this wrong.
You can only do it or not do it.

Focus on your breathing filling you up
and hitting every cell of your body with brightening oxygen.
When your mind wanders,
tug it back by focusing
on that body of water and your breathing.

Keep gently bringing your mind
back to how your body feels,
and how your mind responds to that beautiful water.

Ten minutes a day is the recommended time;
start with the magic three.
It gets easier.

Intention:
Remember— you are clearing off that table.
Quieting the mind is a part of this.

# 67. Explore Possibilities

It is Possible You are Everything You need to Be.

Anything is possible.
When doing this exercise,
don't go down some macabre, sad trail.
We are focusing on the blank page of your mind.
We want to rewrite our story to be 100 percent ours—
not influenced by the news,
your mother, your siblings,
and especially not Hazel from the tenth grade.

What is true for you?
Do you want to explore crystals,
but they seem hokey?
A spiritual path is *completely* hokey
and no one's business but yours.
Do you want to investigate ancestral magic?
Do you love Jesus? Mohammad?
Find the practice of Buddhism fascinating?
Maybe there is a Guru you grew up with.
Maybe none of that is real for you,
and instead you want to explore the mind/body connection.
It may all be the same thing!

The point is, this aspect of your life is vital.
It is the glue that holds the rest of this together.
Don't skip this part.
You got this, find your Path.

Intention:
What do I believe?
What do I want to believe? Believe that.

## 68. Don't be a Hater

Super Hard to do some days.

Now that you are investigating yourself, you can't go around hating on things that are different! If you stay on a traditional Path, you understand that everyone struggles, and everyone has to find their own way. Your mental health is highly dependent on letting go of control. This is particularly hard if you fundamentally disagree with someone else's Path.

The important thing to realize is it's none of your damn business what they do. Thinking about their Path only brings you added stress that you seriously don't need. Look at others within your own loving paradigm, and allow them to have the Journey they need to have.

Within our polarizing society, it is important to understand that, even if we disagree with a person's spiritual and social paradigm, they aren't evil.

The most amazing thing you can do to influence the world is live by shining example. The more you understand your own life and loving paradigm, the more you are able to affect change for the better. Whatever that may be.

Look at how you see others. If your gut twists when you think about people who are different than you, you are the problem. This is so important to identify in ourselves — no matter what side of the fence we live on. Start stripping away at hate, and bring on the compassion!

Intention:
What or who do I hate? Why?
Can I instead act from a place of compassion?

# 69. Find Common Ground

*From here, the hate will disipate.*

The best way to eliminate hate is to find something within another person's reality that you can either relate to or feel compassion for. When faced with extreme hatred, all the great spiritual leaders did this.

Why? Because doubling down on hatred doesn't solve the problem. It does absolutely zero for your mental health. Not to mention, it usually reinforces their belief system. Don't let that kind of hate win. Don't let your own hate win. Not everyone is on the Path. When you allow for others to be themselves and focus on your own Journey, it is easier to say without malice, and with all sincerity, "that is a shame".

We are all affected by the echo chamber of our own thinking. We gravitate toward news and social media that reinforces our beliefs. The documentary *The Social Dilemma* tells us this is not only a reality, but a calculated cocoon that keeps us safe from broader thinking.

You can always find Common Ground with someone who's religion, or lack of religion, or politics are diametrically opposed to yours. Be truly noble. Fail at this a thousand times, because we are not perfect.

Everything takes practice.

Intention:
Can I bond with others who think differently than me?

## 70. Let Someone Know How You Feel

My Sciatica is acting up -
And the Rheumatism is Kicking in!

No; not physically.
When you are young, feelings are wrought
with romanticism or hatred.
That isn't what this means.

When someone does something kind,
funny, or above and beyond—
take a minute to recognize them.
Perhaps, not in the condescending
pat-on-the-head-atta-boy way,
but tell them with gratitude.
This keeps you humble, while giving them a boost.

It is all-around positive for everyone.
Do this without thought and often. Do it simply.
Tell that girl her shoes are awesome.
Tell that co-worker she is killing it,
and you are so grateful and impressed by her.
Tell that kid they should go for it;
nothing is stopping them.

Pay attention to what you are impressed by
and do it yourself.
This gets you outside of your head and feeds your soul.
It's a great exercise in positive lifestyle.

Intention:
Can I find ways to lift up those around me?

## 71. Pay Attention To How You Live Your Day

As it drags on in endless monotony?

What do you prioritize in your day?
Does it feed your mind, body, and soul?
Or, is it a series of oppressive tasks?

When you are on your Path,
it is important to prioritize one thing every day
that feeds more than just your kids.
Or the pets. Or your boss. Or that bitch in your head.
You don't have to be perfect at everything every day.
This is the Journey,
and you are not in it for the Destination.
You are lucky enough to be in it at all!
Treat those days like the gifts they are,
and spend a little time every day
making sure you feed the Holy Trinity.

Mind ~ Body ~ Soul

You can do a 3-minute meditation and a 15-minute workout. Or meal plan for the week and say a prayer of gratitude at bedtime. Do you have extra time today, but you are crazy exhausted? Sleep without guilt. Get a massage. Binge a little TV!
Tomorrow, you start again with realistic expectations.
We fail when we try to bang out everything in one day, and then expect to keep that up every day. That will not happen.
So give yourself the love you extend to others.

Intention:
How will I feed my Holy Trinity today?

## 72. Admit When You Have Done Something

This is tricky.

If your nature is to take responsibility for every little thing,

KNOCK THAT CRAP OFF.

First and foremost,
you need to admit when you have done something good.

If, on the other hand, your nature
is to be defensive and angry,
stop and think before you react.

Breathe, and figure out where you fit into the equation.
Take responsibility for your part in an interaction,
even if the person you are dealing with is an asshole.

If you are situationally both of these people:
stop, breathe, channel empathy,
and try to see your actual part in the interaction.
Don't say sorry for everything. But also, don't lash out.
Both are extreme, dramatic reactions.
You are on the Path now.

You can say,
"Well shit, I gotta work on that."
Or you can say,
"Hmmm, that person is struggling, but that is on them."
Neither reaction will take away from your mental health,
and both help you move forward in a positive direction.

Intention:
Can I admit when I have acted positively or negatively?
Can I tell the difference?

## 73. Drop the Fear

*"Fear is the mind killer."*
*~ Bene Gesserit litany against fear*
*from Frank Herbert's Dune.*

More than anything in our lives, fear inhibits us.
It's at the root of every evil. Fear makes us hate. Fear stops us from being authentic. Fear prevents us from making choices. Fear places us in a box, and makes us worship false gods that we believe will keep us safe. Time to break down those walls of fear, and walk out into the big wide world of possibility.

Fear is the mind killer. When we live a life that is based on fear, we aren't actually living. We are just existing. Do we honestly think that is what we are meant to do? If we worship a god that makes us fear everything, maybe find a different way to relate to god. God is great, but if your god is an asshole, you aren't really worshipping god — you are worshipping fear.

If you aren't religious, but are fear driven because you are afraid of "being found out for who you really are" — stop.
Understand that only you have the power to condemn you. Live authentically. The world isn't a vampire, and it won't suck you dry. Only that Bitch In Your Head has the power to do that. If you learn to love the person inside of you more than anything else, you get to develop Courage. Courage allows you to live your life authentically. Authenticity allows you to benefit others. This is how we affect the world! It starts with you. Drop the fear, become the best you.

Intention:
Do I live in fear? What do I fear?
How can I change the way I see these things?

## 74. Try The Thing That Scares You

I could Never!

But you can. Seriously, you can!
We are rewriting the old script, and creating a new one.
This is how we train ourselves to become
the person we want to be.
One little victory at a time.

Maybe this involves applying for a new job.
Maybe it is simply telling that guy
that is always leaving his shit at your desk to pick it up.
Maybe it is being honest with your sexual partner
about what you like in bed!
Maybe it's flying.
Talking to someone different than you.
Admitting trauma. Going to counseling.
Getting help in general. Trying yoga.

Think logically about how ridiculous the fear you have is.
Is the Yoga God going to come down and smite you
for not being able to hold a pose?
Is your life going to fall apart because you got help?
Is your sexual partner, the person with whom
you share your most vulnerable moments
and presumably loves you,
going to NOT want you to enjoy your time together?
You see, life is a series of choices.
We get to make the choices that move us forward.
We are the only ones standing in our way.

Intention:
What am I afraid of doing? How can I do it?

## 75. Look Into A New Way Of Thinking

Don't Knock it 'til you try it.

If you are struggling in life,
your ideas are probably the ones that got you to this point.
Maybe try someone else's ideas!
They aren't going to be any better or worse
than the struggles you already face.

If you have always done something a certain way,
and it is not working for you, why keep doing it that way?
We call this bashing your head against the wall.
The blood and brain bits aren't pleasant! Stop!
There are about a trillion books and guides in this world
to help you through everything you can imagine.
There is also this amazing resource called — the internet.

Be open to the fact that other people may be able to help you.
Look into the way people struggle successfully.
See the results honestly.
Not fad diets, not trendy pills, or quick fixes.
These are never the answer.
Look around and begin this struggle, whatever it is, differently.
Ask for help. Ask for answers.
Then, and this is the important part, be open to the answers.
It would be easier if we could have everything magically
solved for us, but the Journey requires commitment.
That doesn't mean it has to be horrid.
It can just mean different.
Different is definitely a good thing,
if what you are doing isn't working.

Intention:
Do I fight the solution? Can I open my mind
to hear answers that are different than mine?

## 76. Scrape The Muck Out Of Your Soul…

Like Black Tar out of a Smoker's lungs.

This isn't a one-time thing.
Although, a good initial few months with a counselor
can really scrape away some years of mucked up thinking.

When you review your day,
make sure to not live in the poor choices.
Look at them. Catalogue how you can handle them better.
Then, throw the regret out the window.
Wallowing is only second to fear
in the Soul Destroyer Rating Scale.

You cleared off the table,
but no doubt, you will continue to throw trash on it.
No kitchen stays orderly and clean for any length of time.

The same is true for our mental health.
This is a lifetime thing.
Keep cleaning out the negativity,
and breathing in all the good, fresh, clean positivity.
It can become a great habit
to immediately process a choice.
If you do that, you are constantly growing.
Growth is how we move forward on the Path.

Intention:
Do I keep checking in with myself?
Do I wallow in the negativity?

# 77. Feel It

## DON'T MASK IT

We have come to a place where we have remedies for every single thing. Remedies can help ease pain, heartache, anxiety, and loss, but it is important, also, to learn how to feel things fully. It is important to feel through the pain.

When we constantly mask or ignore how we feel,
we don't learn how to actually deal with the feelings.
We don't develop any grit. All things take practice,
and learning how to cope with negative feelings
is a vitally important part of moving forward.
Left unaddressed these emotions
will come out sideways and toxic.

You need to develop coping mechanisms to help you through the pain. These coping mechanisms include all things:
breathing, crying, counseling, exercise,
and everything in between.

Know this: you are not unique in your fears, pain, anxiety and shame. It feels like you are the only one who feels all of these things so intensely. You are not. The great thing about being on the Journey, is that it allows you to be connected with everyone else, instead of being an island. We may be special in our own way, but we are not so unique as to feel pain "better" than others. Know your pain is real, but learn how to respond to it in healthy ways. Learn how to feel without it shutting down your ability to function. In order to do this, you need to practice. Feel that pain for what it is.

Intention:
Do I allow myself to feel through the pain
so that I may grow stronger?

## 78. If You Knew Everything You Would Be God

Don't let anyone tell you
How to Believe.

Nowhere in this book will it ever tell you to Believe a certain way. Be wary of anyone that says they have all the answers. Your Journey is personal. We have been told by so many people, organizations, and religions how to do every little thing. What a relief to know that you don't have to know everything. That, in the not knowing, you will grow to understand. This is the exciting part about being on the Journey: the growth. That, even when you have moved forward and evolved, there is so much more to look forward to.

It's your Journey. Nobody knows what your next move has to be. This is a personal relationship with yourself. This also opens your mind so that you can constantly take in new information. You can believe one thing, learn something new, and, because you aren't God, you can change your mind.

The beauty of this kind of thinking is that it prevents you from hating or judging things you don't understand. This is your Journey, and no one can tell you what you have to be. The point is to be on the Journey.

You are Free!

Intention:
Do I judge things that I don't understand?

# Wake Up

## 79. You Are Loved

*"If you can't love yourself, how in the hell*
*you gonna love somebody else?"*
*~ RuPaul*

There are likely a few people we can count on to love us.
Sometimes more, sometimes less.
That is truly not the important part of the equation.
How can we expect people to love us,
if we don't love ourselves?
If we truly want to evolve,
*this* will be a huge part of the equation.

If you don't feel this way about yourself, work on it!
Say daily affirmations in the mirror
because, dammit, you are actually worth it!
Even though we face these problems with humor,
the truth is, so many of us don't see ourselves as worthy.

You are Sooo Not Alone!

Start with that tiny piece of yourself that you know is good, and build on that. You are the most important person in your equation, why would you not prioritize yourself? Whatever jack-ass in your past planted those seeds of self-doubt and rejection, process through that tout de suite. This is vital to your Journey. You are not to blame for your self-perception, but you are responsible to change it because self-hatred of any kind is just plain abusive. You are the last person that needs to be abusing you.

Rise up sisters, be the phoenix you are meant to be!

Intention:
Am I abusive to myself? Do I know how to really love myself?

## 80. Accept Care

Oh – they don't REALLY WAnt to help...

Here it is: if they really don't want to help, that is on them.
Plus, why would someone offer to help
if they don't want to help. Accept the help.
Now, don't be dependent.
Don't abuse those around you.
As with all things, there is balance here.

There is no benefit to being helpless.
So, if that is your nature, heed the balance.
If your nature is more, "I can do it!",
to the detriment of your own health and safety,
take the help!

Most of the time when people want to help,
they feel relieved that they can actually do something.
Give them a chance to help.
Allow them to help in the best way they can,
and then let it go.
Controlling how they help is not exactly a healthy response.
And because we actually don't know everything,
how they help may be just fine.
This kind of micromanagement makes us crazy
and does nothing to foster relationships in our lives.
Learn how to accept help, accept responsibility,
and free ourselves from the God complex
of micromanagement.

You may just learn that the other way
to do something is pretty cool too.

Intention:
Do I know how to accept help?

## 81. Be Amazed

*Cue the sweeping music.*

We control our responses.
We are shaped by our early exposures and enculturation.
This can give us a rather jaded attitude toward certain aspects of the world around us. Maybe we were taught to hate the city, or the country. Neither is correct. Neither has perspective.
Both are truly amazing, and it is at your disposal to see that.

If we walk around judging entire aspects of the world, we miss out on the freaking unbelievable, beautiful complexity of it. You choose to respond this way now. Because you have cleaned out all the past muck, you can see the world anew. You can revisit old, entrenched perceptions, and experience awe.

Seriously. Look at the road you go down every day and start to really see it. Notice something new about something that you have seen a thousand times. Open your eyes and open your heart.

Let the ordinary be extraordinary. It's not like you have to get all weird or anything. You don't have to stare at a stink bug sitting on the wall for 75 minutes and say things like "Man, look at the jointed legs. It's so brown, but kind of black too." And so on. That is a hallucinogenic Journey, and that isn't this book! We are talking about stripping down the limitations of your past, and seeing more to the world than the walls that were built up around it through your childhood and early adulthood. Access the world through filter free eyes.

Be amazed.

Intention:
Can I look at the world around me with new eyes?
Can I choose to let myself see things with more awe?

## 82. Wonder At Others

How does she make it out of bed in the morning?!

The same kind of enculturation that shapes our response to the world, shapes our response to others. When we are young, we believe there is only one way to do, be, and see things.

As we get older, we see that people are different from us. But, do we learn to celebrate that? Do we offer them the same grace and consideration we are supposed to give ourselves? Do we place them in the "other" box, and never take time to learn about the way they live their lives? This is how we make connection. We start by being amazed at all the different ways to believe, celebrate, cook, raise kids, relax, entertain, and live. If you don't like something, don't immediately discount it. Try to see it from the perspective of someone else. You don't have to like it, you just have to wonder at it.

If someone is less fortunate and doesn't have all the opportunities that you had, you can be amazed at their adaptability or creativity. If someone is from a really different place than you, you can learn about their culture. Every person has a little something to wonder at. The challenge is when you really don't relate to them. We all struggle with this. The point is to try. We won't always be walking, angelic visions of grace, but we can always be a little kinder. In that process, we might see something new and wonderful.

Intention:
Can I rethink how I see people in my life?

# 83. Engage

Not a Star Trek reference –

But it is a jump start to life.
Nothing happens if we sit and watch our life go by.
What if we were able to do amazing things
just by starting to do little things.
This is actually the whole point of getting on the Path.

When we sit on the outside and watch others we think,
'I wish I could do that'. We simply need to start doing it!
When amazing things don't happen, we need to recommit.
We always need to be engaged on the Journey.
This is the amazing part. We decide to do little things.
They lead to bigger things. We fail at some things. We learn.
We do the things again, but differently.

The point is if you do nothing, nothing happens.
So just start. Commit to trying. Develop the skill of trying.
Develop the Teflon needed to fail and start again.
Always engage with the idea of a better self.
No matter what, stay commited to the Journey.
Does that mean your entire life needs
to be a nips-out, fiery rush to some imaginary finish line?

No!

Because we are on the Path, and that isn't the way.
Engage and move forward.

Intention:
Am I committed to staying engaged in taking care of myself?

# 84. Wait For It

But– I don't want to!

All this engaging, doing, committing, self-caring
does not lead to an overnight success story.
That is not why you are doing these things.
You are Journeying so that you can find more peace,
contentment and, yeah,
maybe a little more success in your life.
But guess what?
You can't make yourself perfect,
and you can't force a life on yourself.
So, have some damn patience with yourself.
This is a never-ending story.
What you do to self-improve is a part of your life.
In the meantime, brick-by-brick, you get to build
yourself into an extraordinary person.
It happens by default while you are rising from the ashes.
As you begin to open up and commit to compassion,
you get to know yourself a little better.
From here you get to be whatever you want.
This kind of commitment doesn't happen overnight.
How fast it happens isn't the important part.

You get to be happier in the meantime,
and that is what the Journey is all about:
the value of each day, not the destination.

Intention:
Can I be patient with myself?
Can I enjoy the me that I am living as today?

## 85. Do One Thing

### Is this a 'Just Do It' Kind of thing?

Well, kinda.
Sometimes we are beat down,
and can't see the forest from the trees.
We may be struggling with depression,
a recent defeat, loss, or any number
of mind numbing, anxiety producing, or painful experiences.
Stay in bed? Maybe. But make sure to do one thing.
Just one thing! That will begin the process
of pulling you up from those doldrums.

That night, write that one thing down, and be grateful.
The next day —
keeping trying to do something
until you can step back
on that illustrious Path we talk so much about.
Don't beat yourself up while you are down.

Just do one thing. Then maybe do another.
And if you can't do more than that,
make sure the one thing you do is ask for help.
When we struggle, the phone is like a 5,000 pound device
that we won't pick up to literally save our lives.

Do one thing. Then when we feel better and are back to walking down the Path, develop a plan for the next time we feel down. Because, when we are feeling low, that isn't the time to suddenly develop useful coping mechanisms. Those need to be on reserve. When we are stuck, in general, a good rule is to do one thing. Then do the next.

Intention:
Do I have tools to help cope with the hard times?

# 86. Choose Faith

This really isn't RELIGIOUS!

Believe in something.
Shepard Book from the movie *Serenity* said,
*"I don't care what you believe in, just believe in something."*
Faith is required for belief.
When you are developing tools to help you cope,
hard faith in something is a great fall back.

You can believe in the science of meditation.
You can believe in Jesus.
You can believe in your ancestors,
a guru, the Dali Lama, Mohammad,
the Spirit, the Triple Goddess,
your grandma's shrines, breathing techniques,
exercise endorphins, yoga.

The point is, if you don't have something to fall back on in hard times, you will rely on yourself. It's not a great plan. You are the one who has landed in a hard time. Something outside of your best intentions needs to help you deal with this moment. That is faith.

Believe hard, because the harder you believe the more you can depend on this as a savior during the low times. Without the pre-existing condition of a well-established relationship with something outside yourself, you are left hanging in the wind. There is nothing there to guide you out of darkness. Don't judge the idea of it, choose to explore it. Choose faith.

Intention:
Do I believe in something?
Does it help me through hard times?

## 87. Learn About Whole Food

No- Not the Grocery Store.

Let's get used to the idea that our body is part of our mental health. Processed sugar not only slows our cognitive abilities, but is as addictive as alcohol. Fast food has added sugar on a level that rivals grandma's homemade caramels.

I am not saying you have to go all *Skinny Bitch* perfectly tomorrow. But by all means: read their book. Watch a documentary. Soak in the info. If you read all of the books ten years ago, read some new ones. Food is the disease of the 21st century that we don't talk about. So what? You are on a Path, and you get to explore whatever you want. Food is just another one of the things. If you suck at it, learn a little bit more. If you are addicted, admit it and get help. Are you too restrictive and controlled? Same thing: admit it and get help.

Can we stop with the shame thing already? If you have cancer, you aren't running around in shame avoiding help. You get treatment. Take some time to develop an actual understanding of food, and maybe begin a healthier relationship with it. Food can wreak havoc on the Holy Trinity. Learn and relearn what you are eating.

Remember: nowhere on this page does it say you should eat perfectly, and be an austere saint with a perfect body. That is not the Path. Just learn what is healthy, and keep on learning.

Intention:
What do I know besides the calories and fat content of the food I eat? Can I look at food differently? Can I grow a better understanding of what I put in my body?

# 88. Get Back On The Path

When you fall off the horse
GET BACK ON—

Don't worry. It's absolutely expected.
We fail at something on our list every day.
But even simple kindness is part of the growth equation.
It is all part of the Journey.

If you really want to do this right,
become okay with falling down.
It's the getting-back-up that is all the fun.
The getting-back-up builds grit.
The getting-back-up creates opportunities.
The getting-back-up is how you learn.

Maybe change course.
Maybe veer in a different direction.
Whatever you were doing before,
do it differently next time. That is the ticket.
Sometimes this is all really clear,
and other times we are fumbling around in the dark.
Remember, the dark days are part of this too.
You don't have to stay in the dark without help.
You are developing tools to help you through those times.

Know that you are not perfect, but you are perfectly you,
and that is all we need. Walk in the dark for a minute,
but don't give up.

Intention:
Am I developing resilience?
Can I see my failures as learning opportunities
instead of punishing myself?

## 89. Access Your Connection

But the gate is so FAR –
& my flight leaves soon!

Mind, body, spirit: the Trinity.
As you start to see yourself as a product of self-care,
you can better understand how everything
you do, say, and eat are related.

How do you access the glue that allows you to tune into your mental and physical health? How do you quiet the mind long enough to understand how your body is feeling?

It's that indefinable thing that we call spirit, soul, endorphins, whatever. The glue is the overarching thing that we need to get in touch with, that helps us calm ourselves, and guides us through hard times. When people say they are coming undone, that is what they are talking about.

Practice connecting with your glue as often as you can.
Develop a simple mantra. Even, "guide me" is enough.
Or, if you prefer, "guide me, Jesus", or "Goddess, guide me".
Dealers choice. Use the saying to help you access that glue.

If you need scientific evidence to do a practice like this, think of meditation as a short cut that allows you quick access to calming hormones. Does it really matter? As long as it works! Whatever it is, make it short enough to repeat so that when you are stressed out, you can say it in your head over and over. This is a mental training exercise. This is prayer.

This is meditation. This is how you do it.

Intention:
Do I have a tool that connects me to the spirit?

## 90. Share In Happiness

### Clap Your Hands!

You are sitting on the couch wondering if you should do fifteen minutes of yoga or eat that pint of ice cream. You get a text from your best friend. She got a promotion that comes with a new car. Your other friend is marrying the man of her dreams. Your sister texts you to tell you she's moving to Shangri-La to live in the fifth dimension with her demi-goddess life partner. Are you feeling supportive or jealous? Either way...do you know what any of this has to do with you? … nothing.

Take a breath and understand how freaking awesome it is that you are surrounded by all this positive energy. Only *you* can choose to make this about you. Only you can see this as taking away from your Journey. It doesn't. You won't be able to share *your* happiness with them if you don't share in *their* happiness. Eliminate all the presumptions about why they are sharing with you and just celebrate. If you are genuinely happy for them, you give yourself the gift of happiness and them the gift of sincerity. Jealousy is a one-way soul nibbler. It eats away at us while not having any affect at all on the other person.

Maybe avoid all of this drama, and just be happy for the ladies and their accomplishments. That is all any of us want when we reach out with news. Share in the happiness. Maybe find out if you can visit your sister in her new home. Soak it up and then do the yoga.

Intention:
Do I truly celebrate
my friends' successes and happiness?

# 91. Wake Up

The hardest part of the day
is the first ten minutes.

Any time we start something new, we struggle.
It is just the way it is.
Experience tells us this is temporary.
Perseverance is largely
just getting through the start of the day.
This period of time is difficult.
Then — it gets easier. We move forward.
Eventually, waking up is easy.
You barely remember how hard it was in the beginning.

Here is the thing,
you have to start your day by Waking up.
If you don't go through that first ten minutes,
there is no rest of the day.

Get up and put yourself out there.
Try the hard things, connect with the fire,
and move through the pain.
It's not a Nike commercial.
You aren't trying out for the Olympic anything team.
Know the initial learning period is temporary.
Know you have some tools to help you get through it.
Know that if you don't start,
you don't get to have the next part
where you aren't struggling.
Wake up, rise up and start something new!

*Then take a nap.*

Intention:
Are you blocking yourself from something because you don't want the beginning? Can you see past that?

# Don’t Stagnate

## 92. Embrace The Difficult

The Buddha said Life is Suffering.

That may be a bit dramatic.
Life is hard. No doubt.
Accepting that everyone has hurdles helps us
realize that we are not alone in this struggle.
It also helps us see that we can either:
live in the difficulties, or we can accept them as challenges.
Now obviously that doesn't apply
when you are struggling with breast cancer chemotherapy.
In that case, we focus on self-care.

But the day-to-day challenges
(and even the greater ones) are there to shape you
into the kind of person you want to be.
The key is to learn how to react to the struggle.
Does everything seem hard and insurmountable
or do you start to bust it down into manageable pieces
and get to work on problem solving?

Whatever is stressing you out and looms large over your life,
it is likely a lot smaller of a problem
than you have currently worked it up to be.
Figure it out.
Build some resilience in the process
and be proud of what you have done.

Every time you conquer a problem you build confidence.
The key is to dig in, and get it done!

Intention:
Do I let myself freeze up over problems? Can I break things down
and attack them that way? Do I understand that
Trying and Doing are what build up my self-esteem?

# 93. Take A Break

Crashing & Burning is not
an efficient way to Stop.

Don't ram your head against the wall.
It happens to us all; we just want to finish this, or that.
That's when mistakes start to happen.
We get careless and we leave a project half-assed.
Respect yourself enough to finish the project
to the best of your ability.
This applies to *all* areas of life.

Give yourself some time and attention.
If you run ragged all the time, you can't be the best you.

*"But what am I supposed to do? I have to….."*

Change your perspective to include self-care.
Can you leave those three loads of laundry unfolded?
Make a soup on Sunday for half the week?
Can you ignore the 100 little tasks
that you think you must do, but really aren't necessary?
Can everyone take care of themselves for a minute?

Can you ask for help?

Take a break and do the things that restore you.
Then come back to it.

Intention:
Do I allow myself time to enjoy my life?
Do I see how this may help me be more productive?

## 94. Run With Wolves

Be outstanding – Without being a fool

We are wild women that are free. This is not the wild women who does whatever she wants. This is about being *fierce.* Anyone can do whatever they want and act the fool.

Find your Pack. Women, or others, that you admire. People that are amazing, interesting, and doing things you want to do. Run the way they do.

Don't see yourself as the victim, see yourself as a Pack member. Even if there aren't many people similar to you where you are — find them in blogs, chat groups, and on social media. Or... move. Be around women that inspire you.

Build others up; let them build you up. This doesn't have to be a literal Pack. They don't even need to know each other! However, they must be daring, fierce, and purposeful. This means that their boldness is largely a product of their purpose. Their fierceness is the momentum that drives them toward their goals.

Being a half-cocked, angry lady that goes off on people because she wants to appear strong is the opposite of strength. It shows complete weakness of character. It is vitriol, and it is unproductive. Seek others who dare to be the women they were meant to be. Seek others who do this without regarding what others think.

They are the fierce ones.

Intention:
Who is in my Pack?

# 95. Dream A Little Dream

*"'Til sunbeams find you"*
*- Mama Cass*

Passion makes the world go round.
No matter where you are in life
you can always reinvent yourself.
Nothing prevents you from becoming the best you,
other than you.

Yes, children, partners, responsibilities—
they are all part of reality.
Despite where we are right now,
life continues, children grow.
We can either start on a Path,
or be in the same place ten years from now.

Dream your dream.
Do what you can to make your dreams a reality.
Even if it will take years to see any progress,
the Journey isn't about the goal. It is about Journeying.

If we stay on a Path
we get to look back at it someday,
but we don't get to if we never start.

  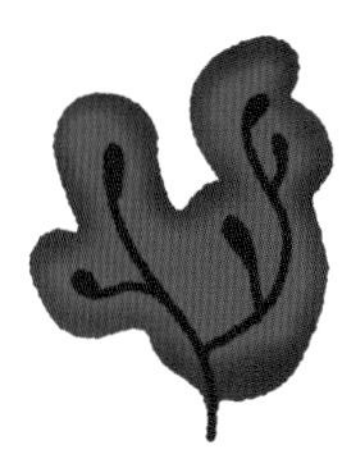

Intention:
What is my dream? Can I do one thing to make it real?

# 96. Make A Plan

Boooringg — zzz

Nothing beautiful in this world
comes without trudging down a Path.

Even snow has to form clouds and get to a freezing state.
It's boring sitting there waiting for the cloud to freeze.
But then — snow gets to free fall to the Earth.

Nurse practitioners in intensive care
get to do all the cool procedures, but there are years of training,
and education, and charting that needs to be done.

Actors have amazing jobs,
but there are auditions and years of trial and error.
Writers have editing, self-promotion;
everyone has critics.

The point is, we have to put in the time to get the rewards.
Sometimes that time sucks.
Commit to the Journey, the time, and the Path.

Single minded determination is what leads you toward a dream.
Waiting for something to happen isn't Journeying.
It is letting the world revolve without you.
Make the decision to make the Path fun.
Because you can!
You can choose to get excited about the next step.
And the next step.
Because you cannot fail at anything
as long as you keep moving forward.

Intention:
Can I become willing?

# 97. Your Plan Isn't The Law

*"We will now discuss in a little more detail*
*the Struggle for Existence"*
*~ Charles Darwin*

Life happens.
In every possible manner, way, shape, and form.
One minute we are living life
with thousands of brands of paper products,
and the next we can't find toilet paper at the grocery store.

So, we re-evaluate.
We change our plans
because we don't want to give our grandma
an infectious disease that could kill her.

Think. Think creatively. Adapt.
Keep on becoming the fabulous you.
This is why we talk about never failing.
Falling yes, but not failing.
Get up, get creative and get going.
The only failure is jumping off your Path,
and allowing the darkness to swallow you.
Do we have dark days — yes.
Sitting in the darkness is okay for a *moment.*
But we have to get back up and do one little thing at a time
in order to stay on the Path.
The plan is allowed to have hiccups and change,
but the Path is always there.

Intention:
Do I allow myself to fall?
Do I get back up without judging myself?

## 98. Believe In Magic

Are we in the seventies?

There are moments in our lives
that are beautiful if we allow them to be.
Sitting in the park and watching a squirrel can be beautiful.
Looking at artwork from our
daughter's kindergarten folder can be beautiful.
An overwhelming sense of peace is beautiful.
That beauty is Magic.

If you can't believe in a higher power,
believe that the unknowable is *everywhere* instead.
Allow your mind to be open to the idea
that we don't know everything,
and this is completely okay.

Freedom from the responsibility of knowing everything,
allows us to See more, Learn more, and Feel more.
Yes, ironically, you end up learning more as a result!
You are freed and now you can become More.

It helps us accept the failures because they aren't wrong.
We don't have to spend all of our time justifying them;
we are too busy learning from them.
Failures aren't stupid.
They are simply steps and stumbles along the way.
This acceptance is how we gain wisdom.
This openess allows the Magic to happen
and the beauty to seep in.

Intention:
Can I open my mind enough to accept beautiful things?

# 99. Learn From New People

*"Do not be afraid, Mithrandir. You are not alone."*
*~ Galadriel, Lord of the Rings*

If we live with a lot of fear,
perhaps we need to listen to a new way of thinking.
Fear is not a healthy state of being. It is a useful situational tool.
In other words, if you are walking along a mountainside,
fear prevents us from carelessly skipping to our death.
But living in fear over world news
or unrealistic self-expectations is destructive.

If we want to make positive changes in the world,
we can't listen to fear. We have to listen
to people who actually make a difference.

This is IMPORTANT.

We need to listen to someone different
than the people creating fear for us.
Shut down the social media,
turn OFF the news, and look around.
Learn from actual humans that aren't selling a product.
Don't listen to what people say, per se.
Look at what they do. Talk is cheap.
If someone is doing something that inspires you, listen to them.
Learn from the people that make a difference.
Even if they think differently than you, learn from that.
If we drop the fear, every situation can teach us something.
We must open ourselves up to new possibilities.

Intention:
Can I open myself up to learn
from someone different from me today?

## 100. Include People

This Isn't Kindergarten!

No, it isn't kindergarten,
and healthy boundaries are an important adult skill.
This is about taking a look around to make sure
that you aren't being cruel through exclusion.
If you feel insecure, you can bet that the majority
of people you are surrounded by feel the same.

It is important to work toward understanding people,
especially if they are different than you.
This breaks down fear and hatred,
and helps to further free your mind.
Simply including a person in a conversation
can be enough to make them feel like an ally to you.

We can all use more love in our lives.
If being inclusive becomes a habit,
then you never have to worry about what people are thinking.
They are thinking you are a good person;
that's what they are thinking!
This in turn helps build your own self-esteem.

Kindness and compassion are ultimately empowering.
They lead you down a more contented Path.

Intention:
Do I show kindness in my life?

## 101. Everyone Is Not Inside Your Head

BUT THEY SHOULD KNOW!

Nope. Nope. Nope. They do *not* know.
If someone is acting as if they don't know what
you are thinking in your head,
even though you think they *should*…they don't.
It is as simple as that.

You can either let situations fester, grow,
and become completely toxic.
Or you can just talk about it.
You can talk about it before it even becomes a huge to-do.
Again, if the person doesn't know, then they don't know.
The rules may be clear on the inside of your eyelids,
but that doesn't help the other person.

You may have thought you expressed yourself clearly before,
but clearly they didn't hear you.
If it is a toxic situation, then boundaries need to be set.
That person isn't going to do that for you.
This comes down to that guttural place of self-care.
Make sure that you are your own best advocate.
Allow yourself the kindness of sharing what you are thinking.
Choose to be transparently you,
and you will never have to wonder
why people don't understand.

Intention:
Can I allow myself to be transparent
about my thoughts with others?

## 102. Celebrate Successes

It's not a Pie!!

*Meaning: we are not in constant competition. If someone has an excess of success, why is it hard to be happy for them?*

Because it is sometimes!

It's human nature. But here is the thing, if we celebrate them, rather than ride them down mentally, we can let them inspire us. Think about that. What would happen if every time we felt ugly inside about someone else's success, we flipped that feeling to inspiration?

What is it that they are doing that makes us feel that way? Likely jealousy. That is a truly useless state of being. We feel it, but instead of feeding that emotion, we can try to see how amazing the person's Journey is, and let that feed our own Journey. They can become one of your Pack. If they are doing something that inspires jealousy, then that signifies they are doing something you want to be doing. Sometimes we don't even recognize this. It may simply be that you are jealous of the way they dress. Or as complex as you wishing you could open a bakery, too.

The thing is, you can do anything you want. Remember, it isn't a pie. Her success doesn't mean you get a smaller piece. Success is infinite in a thousand different ways. You are on a Path that doesn't recognize failure. So, celebrate that bitch's success and go out and do whatever you really want to. You can both have the best life. And that is good for everyone.

Intention:
Do I recognize my own wants and desires
through other's successes?

## 103. Help Others Where They Are At

*"Reach out your hand, if your cup be empty.*
*If you cup is full, may it be again."*
*~ Ripple, The Grateful Dead*

We are all at different places in life.
Helping others is an important part of mental health.
Maybe you are finally running that bakery,
and killing the maxi dress with purple hair game.
To get to that place, you have fallen countless times.
Someone else may still be trapped in fear.
We can't expect that person to jump straight
to the "open their own business
and wear whatever inspires them" place tomorrow.

In order to be a part of this grow-and-give circle,
we have to meet people where they are at.
We can only offer to be of service,
and direct people to the help they need.
We cannot fix them.

We can live by example and respond to their needs,
but we cannot make them see what we see.
The need for people to agree with you,
and to see your truth as their truth,
only leads to pain for you.
Freedom lies in achieving peace and contentment.

Intention:
Can I offer help without needing to fix?

# 104. Don't Stagnate

This may take some practice.
And, yes, that lady who is happy all the time
(but borderline hysterical), may not be truly happy.
Choose to move forward; try to shine through the darkness.

We have hard days.
Recognize that and allow for it.
In a time where there is so much anger and pain, be the light.
Choose to move forward
with all of the good things you want for your life.
Understand that this is a choice.
People aren't naturally happy and content,
they prioritize and work toward it.

Choose to work toward the light.
Choose to move forward.
Choose to believe in yourself.
The actual goal isn't what will bring you joy, it's that choice.

There are always goals, small and large.
The Journey is worth it. Choose not to stagnate.

Intention:
Do I believe in myself enough to move forward?

# Wonder

## 105. Let Your Fear Go

Easy for You to Say —

Why not? Very rarely is what you fear based in any kind of reality. Our fears are developed over time, and they are likely rational (or irrational) responses to something from our childhood, early adulthood, an emotionally abusive person of power in our life, or, yes, the media.

The good news is, we don't have to live in fear. We can identify every fear we have, and bust it down to its origins. If the fear is general like the government, or God, or any number of vague but pressing issues that plague your news feed and mind —know it is not a real fear.

But But But

...nope, not a real fear. Do you think someone who wears a rubber hat every day for fear of being struck by lightning is rational? Look at the odds of these general fears. Our fears around the grand sweeping issues are just as irrational. Dump that fear first. You have no control over the vast majority of these types of fears, and they are an enormous waste of energy.

Next are the fears like being judged, or fear of confrontation. These may be from our past. Figure out why those responses happen, and work with someone to move past them. Then there is the fear of failure. This paralyzing fear doesn't let us move through the Journey. It needs to be conquered. Again, work with someone on these issues. Then let go of that damn fear!

Intention:<br>
What fear inhibits me moving forward?<br>
(If there is a physically abusive person in our life,<br>
Call for help now. 800-799-SAFE).

# 106. Let Something Mysterious In

*"What we lose in our great human exodus from the land*
*is a rooted sense, as deep and intangible as religious faith,*
*of why we need to hold on to the wild and beautiful places*
*that once surrounded us." ~ Barbara Kingsolver*

Something needs to replace fear.
Something needs to seep in and settle deep
where the fear has taken root, and replace it.

There are a million ways
to find deeper meaning, to find mystery.
Believe in something pure and good.
Fear is the opposite of faith,
and takes us away from a place of contentment.

Mystery like this can be found anywhere.
Nature, religion, art, meditation, yoga,
even science can bring mystery to our world.

Having the ability to open up to the Possible,
allows us to grow emotionally as people.
Take the leap of faith and investigate where you put your faith.
If it does not strengthen you, if it does not replace fear,
then maybe it is time to change things up.

Intention:
Can I let go of fear, and let something else in?

## 107. Accept a Miracle

I'm not talking about
speaking in tongues.

If we can allow for mystery,
we can see the world for its possibilities;
we can be amazed at simple things.

Cynicism eats away at our souls,
one bitter moment at a time.
Now, there is nothing wrong
with occasional well-placed sarcasm.
We aren't boring saints without senses of humor.
But maybe open up a bit,
and see the world for its possibilities.

Hone in at least once a day on something
that is truly spectacular.
Be amazed at the Miracle
of electricity, or computing power, or antibiotics,
or whoever the heck thought of epidurals.

Look at the miracle of beautiful artwork,
performances, or poetry that make you laugh or cry,
limitless music that comes from limited notes.

Miracles are really a matter of perspective.
Think of how much joy can be had if we allow for Miracles rather than beat down these simple moments.
Choose to see the world this way a little more often.

Intention:
Can I see Miracles in my daily life?

## 108. Make A List

Get down to it!

Collect tools that help you cope.
Anxiety is the number one psych diagnosis in the world.
We all understand moments of anxiety.
Creating a toolbox that helps you cope
with moments of anxiety will only help you on your Journey.

Lists can organize tasks,
but they can do so much more than that.
Lists can help clarify your thinking.
Lists can help identify irrational thinking.
They can help with decision making.

List people, places, thoughts, or things.
Identify patterns of thinking and go deep.
Or simply make a list to help organize your day.

Add Making a List to your toolbox
to help with anxious moments.

Intention:
Do I have tools to help me cope with the moment? Can I list my emotions when I am anxious?

## 109. Say A Mantra

What the heck is a Mantra?

Mantras are another coping mechanism.
They are a series of words that work sorta like a worry stone. They are a prayer repeated over and over.
Religion has used the concept of mantras
as meditation in every different form.
The most familiar, in western Christian ideology, is the rosary.
Saying a prayer over and over and over
clears the mind and helps calm the soul.

A mantra can be a list of words.
It can be a short prayer.
It can be an affirmation or a motivating statement.
It can be a poem.

Whatever it is, you can say it over and over in your head during stressful moments to create that sense of peace and security. It is another coping mechanism for stress, and it is not without scientific backing. Meditation, in a brief form, is what we are talking about here and science has shown us that meditation can only help. This can be another tool for the toolbox of coping mechanisms. But don't walk around in public constantly mumbling your mantra under your breath — that might not be as effective. Keep this one to yourself and it should serve you well.

Intention:
What could I use as a mantra?

# 110. Accept Other's Beliefs

The middle AGES called
—they want their HATRED BACK.

It is so hard to navigate faith as it is.
We don't need to complicate it
by demanding that everyone see things the same way.

Are you religious? Awesome!
It is so great to have a structure to hang on to
that helps guide your faith and sense of mystery.
Do any of the words:
Muslim, Christian, Jewish, Buddhist, Pagan,
Atheist, Hindu, or Sikh strike an emotive response
that lands in your lizard brain?
Well, good news, you are absolved
of needing to care a whit about another person's belief system.
Last I checked you aren't God, and that is God's business.
If we knew God's will, we would be God.
(Unless of course you are a God, then humble apologies.)
Or if you are atheist and think you know better,
you aren't an all-powerful being either.
The point is — compassion comes with acceptance.
We must have compassion for others.
Look how someone's faith helps them rather than judge it.
If we are busy judging their beliefs,
we are then busy making ourselves miserable.
Focus on improving your own faith
instead of worrying about others.

If the difference or lack of faith in others bothers you,
something is missing for you. Look into that instead.

Intention:
Do I lack compassion for other's beliefs?

# 111. Let Go Of Resentment

If everyone else is an asshole
- you're the asshole.

This is a core concept of getting healthy.
Our minds are skilled acrobats
when it comes to convincing us
that we are, in fact, NOT the problem.
Look at the person in your life
who causes rage to seep out your pores.
Now stop. Really stop.

Look at what you are doing in this equation.
There is something that is causing you
to feel all these feels, and it isn't them.
They are blissfully unaware of how you feel most of the time. The only person causing you grief, is you.

This is usually happening because something about yourself
is interfering with your harmony.
It could be as simple as your ego wants validation,
and this person has really hurt your ego
in a way that perhaps you *feel* is true.
It could be fundamental jealousy.
It could be an unhealthy sense of justice,
as if you have some sort of noble overseer power,
and this person isn't following your rules.
We all do this.

What is our role in this relationship
we spend so much time thinking about?
Once we identify that, we can begin to heal.
Make a list. Get rid of those resentments.

Intention:
What is my part?

## 112. Work Your Body

God - You annoy me.

Right?
But, along with all of the feel good healthy mental stuff,
endorphins don't make themselves.
So, *at least* once a week, push yourself physically.
We are all tired.
So hear this, we don't have to do it well.
Suck at being physical, but be physical. Build some grit.

Don't start with doing everything, every day.
Do not expect perfection.
Know that pain, disease, and emotional health
are all improved by some physical activity.
So, once a week push yourself to sweat.
Do something a little physical more often than that,
but once a week really push it.

Since there is no goal or failure here,
you can plateau until you get inspired to push it again.
You can stop and pick it up again,
but don't let your mind convince you that you can't do this.
You have to. This shit is annoying, but necessary.
Develop a relationship with your body;
one that involves understanding and not judgement.
Who cares what anyone thinks, does, or says?
This is *your* Journey,
and you can do it any way that works for you.
Put on that yoga video and fall over 17 times.
Next week, you fall over 16. It's called progress.

Intention:
Do I really know how important my physical body
is to my mental and spiritual health?

# 113. Sleep

*"Per chance to dream."*
*- Hamlet*

If we are taking the physical activity thing seriously,
this can really aid in the ability to fall asleep.
The brain can wreak havoc on this, however.
All you can do is pay attention to your sleep patterns.

Along with understanding the physicality of your body,
understand how sleep is related to this process.
Be kind to yourself.
If you haven't slept all week
due to work, anxiety, or a new puppy,
let yourself sleep-in one day. Play catch up.
Monitor caffeine, exercise, screen time,
or anything else that affects your sleep pattern.
Just pay attention to how much sleep you get.
Sleep is self-care, and self-care is how
we are able to be of service to others.
Service helps us become mentally and spiritually strong
so we can kick some serious ass on our Journey.

But first, take care of yourself.
Get to know your sleep habits;
get to know the things that affect it.
Are we depressed and sleeping too much?
Then force yourself to move, endorphins can only help.
Either way, begin to understand how sleep affects you.
Kindly give yourself what you need.

Intention:
Am I aware of what I need for sleep? Do I take care of myself?

## 114. Check In On The Mystery

Keep Practicing faith in Something.

Much of this Journey requires some daily maintenance.
Since we cannot walk the Path perfectly,
we sometimes think we can't do it at all.
45 second daily check-ins in the morning and at night
can be enough for you to really have some positive changes.

Check in on that Mystery, that thing you put your faith in.
If that is, indeed, scientific then look at thc mysteries
of undiscovered realms and understand
how small your role is in the universe.
The important thing here is to practice both humility and awe.

There is a clear brain reboot that happens
when people find religion.
We all know someone who has turned their life around
because they bought into something.
Who are we to knock the science behind that?

If you have a faith in something already,
focus on the part that inspires you
and creates that sense of awe.
There is already enough negativity and hate in the world.
Choose the mystery that helps you.

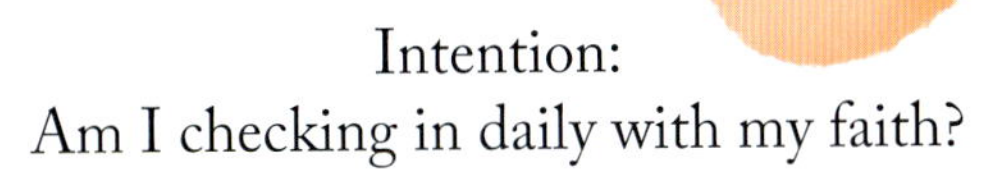

Intention:
Am I checking in daily with my faith?

## 115. Do the Little Things For Yourself

Because Sister, no one else will.

Take a minute this week
to make sure you do something you love.
If you are too busy — schedule it right now.

These habits of self-care are how we become stronger.
If we skip these things to take care of others,
we are teaching others how to treat us.
This can slip us into the dreaded "victimitis" habit,
and that slippery slope is deadly.

If every other thought inside your head
relates to how you suffer, you have really learned
to treat yourself poorly.
That, my dear sister, is entirely your fault.
As an adult, you have the choice to say no.
You have the choice to spend a night free of responsibility.
You have the choice to pamper yourself.
Not all the time, every day, but enough.
It is so important to understand
that no one is responsible for your happiness except you.
If you commit, just a little bit,
to self-care and maintenance,
you create habits that benefit not only yourself,
but those around you.
Your daughters will learn how to be kind to themselves.
The people in your life will see that you know yourself,
and will treat you with the respect
with which you treat yourself.

Intention:
Do I care enough about myself to care for myself?

# 116. Love Differently

Blah-Blah-Blah-

Scorn is everywhere.
Many of us have passion for what we believe in,
but we do it at the expense of a piece of our soul.
It isn't that we have to be completely without fault,
but maybe try a little harder to love your enemy.
Besides, when has hatred ever been the right way
to teach people about a different way of thinking?

We can hear people's views without hatred,
without cultural centrism, without scorn and maybe,
just maybe, they will hear us too.
I guarantee they won't hear you if you are full of hate.
They will only remember the feeling you left behind.

When someone is causing you stress on a pathological level,
spend a few minutes every day
trying to wish them well in your mind.
You can pray for them. You can meditate on their well-being.
You can simply imagine better things for them.
Not immediately, but soon enough, you will find
they aren't consuming your head space the way they did before.

This is the freedom of loving rather than hating.
Change is more likely to happen in your life with love.

Intention:
Can I love my enemy?

## 117. Wonder

*I wonder where this one is going -*

The pain of anxiety, depression, loss, hatred, and fear
are things that cause us grief in this world.
Over and over in history
people have found ways to replace these trials
with a sense of wonder in something.

God is the most common theme here, but not the only one.
Buddhism relies on a more pragmatic understanding
of the world, but no less wondrous.
Knowing that we are all on a Journey, and that we cannot
possibly know what we don't know —
is enough to leave us in a state of amazement if we let it.
It doesn't matter one little bit if it is real.
That is the part that is so freeing.
It is really your peace-making belief system and no one else's.
So, if it works for you... that is real enough.

No matter what, believe in something,
and let that thing help you find
a modicum of peace in this crazy world.

Intention:
Can I find something for myself that is awe inspiring?

# Get Back Up

## 118. Feel The Pain

Whatis this? A sign in a high school locker room?

No, not that kind of pain.
We are talking about going *through* the pain.
Letting painful moments wash through us
rather than burying them;
letting those moments bring us to our knees if we must.
If we don't, the way they come out sideways is much worse.

Get that counselor, therapist, life coach on speed dial,
and get to work on that past trauma. No excuses.
This is how we do it.
Nothing will change without facing it first.
Going forward, you can feel the pain
because you are gaining tools to help cope with that.
You no longer have to pretend
to be an automaton without normal human emotions.
Or you no longer have to fall apart at the falling of rain.
Both are unhelpful, extreme, and destructive.

You are on a Path. Pain will happen.
Look at the tools you have,
and pick some out for dealing with it.
Be kind to yourself. Don't live in the misery.

Intention:
How do I handle pain?

# 119. Find A Way

## Google Maps?

Sometimes we are paralyzed by the challenge before us.
Hoping that someone else will handle it
is not good for our long-term mental health.

Identify how others have done this before you.
Very few things we face are unique.
If we think they are, we should
probably squash that kind of thinking.

Uniqueness separates us from others.
Seeing ourselves and our situations as "different"
takes us away from solutions.
Understand that others have done this, and you can too.
Ask for help, advice or guidance.

Another thing to squash is "feeling stupid".
We are all stupid about things until we learn about them.
Feeling stupid only ends when we allow ourselves
to feel vulnerable and face the answers.
Then, we don't feel stupid.
We feel empowered.

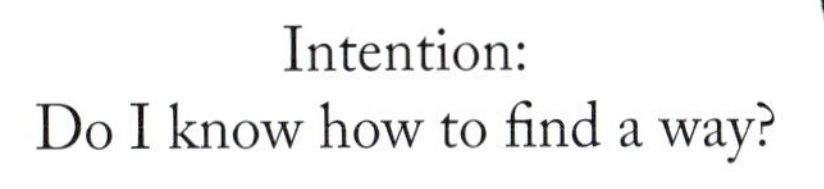

Intention:
Do I know how to find a way?

## 120. Keep Trying

*"Real change, enduring change happens one step at a time."*
*~Ruth Bader Ginsberg.*

Life is hard.
The way we get to the easy parts is to keep trying.
Try again.

Now, don't bang your head against the wall
trying the same thing again and again
to the point of mental health exhaustion and despair.

Try differently.
Try ten different ways.
But keep trying.
Eventually you get to have success!

That is the key.
Not trying is the only way you don't win.
Sometimes we learn so much in the trying
we completely change our direction.
That is really okay! Trying is what led us there.

Intention:
Do I give up too soon?

# 121. Review

Is life a test?

Not a test you can fail,
but certainly one we can learn from.
When faced with a challenge, we can look back
on our lives, and see how we handled a similar situation.

This can be important, not necessarily to give us answers,
but to guide us on how we either do or don't
want to move forward.
We learn so much more from our failures
than when success comes easily.
Don't forget to let that guide you.
Don't forget to not let that frighten you either.

Remember falls are only failures
if we don't let them guide us through the next challenge.
Let our past frame our future.
Let it ultimately lead to the success we want in life.
Remember that when we trip in the future,
this will eventually teach us how to kick ass later on.

Intention:
Do I use past mistakes to guide future decisions?
Do I do that without letting fear interrupt my progress?

# 122. Revamp

*"Remake, Revise"*
*~Merriam Webster*

Bank of America claims the honor
of being the first bank to transition
to computers from paper in 1950.
Hospitals in the U.S. did not transition to computer charting
until well over a half a century later.

Revamping a plan will often
leave people kicking and screaming.
Those people are wasting time.
When a plan needs to be revamped,
don't wait 60 years to do it.
All that does is delay the inevitable
and create unnecessary chaos.

If your plan isn't working for you, change it.
Remake the plan into something that will work.

Look around;
see how others achieve the results you want and then adapt.
The only one you are hurting
by staying on a course that isn't working — is you.

Intention:
Am I fighting change in my life?

## 123. Renew

After all that falling, revamping, & fraying — Time for a Break.

We are not machines that can get up
and repeat the same shit day in and day out.
That can be soul sucking.

Do something in the midst of your chaos
to keep your soul fresh.
Book club, face mask, yoga class, dance lessons,
hike, ski, boat, swim, game, bird watch.
Do the thing that makes you breathe a little easier.
Don't know what that is? Try new things.

Remember, only you are going to take care of you.
Look around and embrace a bit of fun.
Embrace a little relaxation. Even if it's 15 minutes.
You cannot stay on the Path if you don't take time for you.
Laugh at yourself. We are eternally hilarious.
Why in the world shouldn't we enjoy that?
Renew, enjoy, and get up again.

Intention:
Am I making sure I take time for myself?
Am I making sure I laugh?

# 124. Allow Others To Fall

Control is an Illusion

Dear people who love to control every aspect of your life:
Are you miserable?

The only control we have
is control over *our* actions and reactions.
We are constantly trying to control outcomes
that we actually have no control over.
This goes for world politics as well as our son's hockey game.

People are different.
Some are very organized.
For others, it is an accomplishment if they hang up their coat.
The best we can do is express our needs in a relationship clearly.

We cannot control what another person does.
Sometimes, we need to stand by while they struggle.
Offer help, yes, but, mostly,
wait for them to get through their trial.

Wasting your energy on trying to control others' outcomes,
behaviors or inherent personality traits
leads to a lot of misery for both of you. Let go.
Let them have their Journey and their Path.
Support them, love them,
but let them fall where they will
so they can have the awesome opportunity to learn to fly.

Intention:
Do I try to control others in my life?

# 125. Take The Mulligan

GOLF - Really?

Sometimes pride works hard against our own self-interest.
We will bash our head against the wall
trying to say, "I can do it".
When people offer help during a struggle, take it.
Of course, don't pathologically work against
your own self-interest to depend on others.

No, this is about humility and ego.
Say we face a challenge,
and we are trying to do everything to move forward.
We are getting back up, revamping, using all the tools,
and we still aren't getting there.

Someone comes along and says
"Hey, here — take this solution from me".
Take it. Your work isn't invalidated because you were given help.
You are being given something in *addition* to all your work.

Your pride and ego can work against your own self-interest.
In this case, take the Mulligan.
Use the resource, and springboard to a better place.
No one can take your work away from you.
No one can block your Path except you.

Life is hard enough as it is without us blocking ourselves!

Intention:
Do I let my ego interfere with my progress?

# 126. Walk In Beauty

I'm afraid we are a 70's Shampoo Ad.

Taking a little time to see beauty in your day
doesn't mean you have to be some simpering,
fuzzy brained, stoner, flower-child.

Taking a little time to see beauty
will soften some of those harsh edges
that make us quick to anger; even quicker to hate.
Even if you have to carry some kind of pressed flower
in your pocket to remind you that beauty exists, do that!
We must allow ourselves to celebrate the beauty
in the world around us, otherwise what is the actual point?

Beauty shines through that coworker who always takes time
to see how you are doing, even when it annoys you.
Beauty shines through that calm, jovial worker
at the grocery store who asks you about the leek you bought.
Beauty shines through the architecture
of that building on the corner, or that tree on the sidewalk,
or the damn screensaver that Hal has on his monitor
that you find yourself staring at all the time.

Beauty is a matter of perspective, and taking the time to see it.
Breathe; take a minute to see the beauty.
Soften the edges just a little bit.
Life is easier this way.

Intention:
Do I take time to appreciate simple beautiful moments?

## 127. See Good

Define good…

And that is the point.
Good is subjective, just like beauty.
Sometimes people are *trying* to be Good,
and inadvertently offend or hurt.

Instead, see their Good intention.
One, because it makes you more peaceful in your presentation.
And, two, because it makes people more receptive to feedback.
Resolution can happen when we see good.
If we walk around presuming everyone is ugly on the inside,
that only shows that we are feeling ugly on the inside.
Nothing good comes of that.

See the good in people,
and try to let them see the good in you.
When we really try to do this,
it has a weird contagion effect.
People will see the good in you, too.
We can all use a little more goodness in our life.

Intention:
Do I question the motivations of those around me?
Do I see good so others can see good in me?

## 128. Eat A Salad

Little random, but okay.

In the midst of working on self-improvement
we must remember the triad of mind-body-soul.
We can't find ourselves in a healthy place
if we are smoking our breakfast, bingeing on fries,
and drinking our dinner.

The chemicals in our body need balance.
The body needs to have some healthy choices to depend on
so it can produce those chemicals in abundance.
Of course, we don't do this perfectly.
But are we even trying?

Food, alcohol, and drugs have become
such easy coping mechanisms.
Ultimately, they don't work.
They will fail us by making some of us food or drug addicts.
(Alcohol, by the way, is a drug).

They will fail us by making us exhausted,
and depleting all the natural happy chemicals
because, well, that is what they do.
They suck us dry of our natural built-in ability to cope.
If you have been abusing your body
with food or drugs regularly for a while,
it will take a while for those stores to build back up.
Give them a minute to do that.
Start with a salad.
Maybe tomorrow try building on top of that healthy choice.

Intention:
Do I use food and drugs as coping mechanisms?

# 129. Fall Down Again

Can we just Stop with this falling talk?!

No! Get used to falling.
It is how we learn.
The more comfortable we are with this,
the more likely we are to succeed.

The key is to center in on learning, not failure.
If we learn, we get better.

Mental health also requires this understanding.
None of us are perfect at this.
We all have those things we did last year,
or as a kid, or yesterday that make us sick to our stomach.
Letting those moments define us — is our choice.

Quick.
Learn from that moment;
don't dwell in the dark places.
This is the key to the Path.

Intention:
Am I comfortable with the process of moving forward?

## 130. Get Back Up

*But I am tired!*

We are all tired.
You are allowed to stay down for a *minute* or *two*.
Staying in the muck — is eventually a choice.
If we need to roll on our sides, ask for some help,
and crawl our way back up, this is what we must do.
Get out of the mud any way you can, then, start anew.
The alternative is to stay in a dark place,
dwell there forever, staying stagnate in our lives,
wondering if there could be more.

Get used to Getting Back Up.
Eventually, this habit will lead to amazing things.
There is always more to do, or see, or be.
Malcontent is bred like moldy bread in a drawer:
we don't move forward; we stay in one place too long.

Try something different.
Try a different way, a different direction.
But get up and get back on that Path!

Intention:
How can I get back up and get back on the Path?

# You Are Perfect

## 131. Accept The Imperfections

This shit is Perfect...
What are you talking about?

We all have things that are difficult to accept about ourselves.
*Some* stuff we don't like we can change.
Hooray.

Other things are... just the way we are.
Maybe your hair is thin, maybe you are short,
maybe you are tall, maybe you have a forgetful nature,
or maybe your feet are big, pores are large, ears hang funny.

We can spend years over-analyzing what we perceive as faults. We can turn that frown upside down; lie about how we feel.
Or, we can stop obsessing on the negative and heal from it.
Really.

Everyone has shit that isn't perfect.
Accept the things you don't like,
change the things you can,
and focus on the positive.

Journeying
isn't about being perfect,
it's about moving forward.

Intention:
Do I focus too much on negative things about myself?

## 132. Change What You Can

Don't be your own
Worst Enemy—

What about the things we *can* change?
Unhealthy habits, hair color, the way we dress,
talk, relate, our education, our job, our mental health.
If we want, we can change!

There is nothing more self-limiting
than a sentence that begins with,
"I wish I could be more like…."

You can be better than that Dammit!

The thing to really understand,
is that it doesn't happen overnight.
You change one small freaking piece at a time.

It truly is a Journey,
and the Path allows for you to do that in your own way.
Then, one day, you get to look back,
and see how things have evolved for you.

You know what changes
when you don't change the things you can?

Nothing—

Intention:
What do I want to begin to change?

## 133. See Beauty In Yourself

*"We all want something beautiful"*
*~ Mr. Jones, The Counting Crows*

Yes, look in the mirror;
see the Beauty there.

See the Beauty in the moments you share with others,
the errands that you run today,
the way you move, the way that you stand,
the way that you think, the way you share,
and the way you exist.

We aren't being unrealistic;
we are choosing to see beauty.
How we define that beauty
defines the beauty in ourselves.

The Journey allows us to have goals
and head toward a healthier, happier state,
but it also insists we work at it.

Without vanity and ego,
we are simply beautiful.

*We are beautiful, just the way we are.*

Intention:
Do I know that I am beautiful?

## 134. Account For The Good Things

*"I've got two turntables and a microphone."*
*~ Beck*

Even if it's just for the cereal in your bowl,
express Gratitude every damn day.

Practice this like it is your religion.
Over time, it becomes the bedrock of happiness.
Understanding Gratitude protects you from "Victimitis".
It protects you from seeing the world as your enemy.
It reminds us that we are all given gifts in this world,
and that we can live in the light of those gifts.

Gratitude is like a suit of armor
that we can wear against depression and anxiety.
It is the antioxidant of the soul.
Be Grateful and be happy.

Intention:
What am I Grateful for today?

## 135. Share The Pain

*How 'bout if I just give it all away?*

Communicate where you are coming from.
If pain is tearing you apart,
and it is coming out sideways —
share the pain.

If you are a terribly private person,
share with a therapist, a counselor, or a trusted peer.
Eventually, pain on the inside will come out any way it can.
Denial of that pain leads to complicated relationships...
and more pain.

It may be a huge risk for you to share this pain,
but it is a guarantee that you aren't actually unique in this pain.
Your Journey may be yours,
but pain is pretty damn universal,
and ten times to one,
others know your pain.

Get it out there,
and maybe you can give it all away.

Intention:
Am I holding on to pain?

# 136. Allow Others In

That's risky – Really Risky.

Maybe with one or two people it is,
but they are probably assholes,
and you don't need them anyway.

Allowing others in on your pain, your past,
or your life is empowering for you, and likely them.
It is only your fear of being judged
that prevents you from making yourself vulnerable.

People will mostly gain their own sense of security
about their Journey
when you take the risk,
and allow people to know who you are.

Over time,
you get to have a pack
of sisters and others who have your back.
It's really a worthy trade off.

Intention:
Can I let go of fear and let people see me?

## 137. Trust

*When I see this faith and trust, it is beautiful.*
*~Frances Ellen Watkins Harper*

Don't live inside your head.
That Bitch will confound you
into all sorts of pathological states.

Better to let others know how you are feeling
than to leave everyone guessing.
If you live in a more transparent state with others,
they don't need to read the memos
on the inside of your eyelids.

They don't shock you with their responses, mostly,
because they know what you are thinking and feeling.
Then when people around you tell you something,
trust they mean it.
Trust that people's intentions aren't evil.
It's not your job to evaluate their Path, so trust them.
Now, of course, we don't mean
the gas lighter, that abusive guy,
or some other narcissist you have floating around in your life.
We mean in your daily relationships.
Trust when someone tells you that you did well, they mean it.
Trust when someone says they want to help, they mean it.
Trust when someone says they want to listen, they do.
Trust is the opposite of guilt.
Learn to trust more and guilt less.

Intention:
Do I trust people enough?

# 138. Create Boundaries

This is about the Assholes.

All this trusting requires clear boundaries.
Don't tell everyone, everything.
Don't let everyone in.
Don't let people hurt or manipulate you.
Create boundaries.
You are not in fourth grade anymore,
and you can stop that girl on the playground from hurting you.

People aren't all healthy,
but our reaction to them is completely under our control.
We can walk away.
We can say things like,
"Why would you say that?"

We can empower ourselves
to be in control of our emotional reactions.
Then we can hear their response.
Maybe we did mishear them.
It is important to be open to that.
Maybe they are jerks.
Either way, you have given the situation
the boundary required to protect yourself.
You don't have to be close to everyone.
You can be kind to everyone,
and still have boundaries.

Intention:
Do I know how to create healthy boundaries for myself?

## 139. Get Physical

*"I want to hear your body talk."*
*~ Olivia Newton John*

Listen, we don't judge on the Path.
If you want to get your exercise horizontally — have at it.
Just remember those boundaries.

Our holy trinity is rearing its beautiful head again:
Mind-Body-Soul.

Sometimes, all this mental health work gets overwhelming
and we need a natural boost.

Endorphin therapy to the rescue!
Break into a sweat for more than a minute.
It is a medication for all the angst in our soul.
At the very least it will make you feel good about yourself.
Do it because, without this habit,
the others are so much harder.
Do it because white wine and a joint are easy,
but inevitably slightly, or entirely, soul crushing.
Just do it.

Intention:
Do I see how exercise is like medication for the mind?

# 140. Eat Well

*"We all eat, and it would be a sad waste*
*of opportunity to eat badly."*
*- Anna Thomas*

Eating with a purpose *today* will help with the blues.
Eating healthy is actually, by definition, self-care.
Care about yourself enough to think it through.

To start:
choose one meal to focus on,
but think about it;
forgive past behavior;
don't make it weird!
Just revel in the beauty
of making one meal that is good for you.

Think about making it a habit,
but don't punish yourself for lack of perfection.
This meal can be a habit over time,
like all the things that are helping you down the Path.
These little things are steps.

In the meantime, you get to focus
on a little self-care today!

Intention:
Do I care about myself enough to make healthy food choices?

# 141. Try, Try Again

*If you fall off the horse, get back on.*

We have the opportunity to grow, or to stagnate.
Growing requires all sorts of attempts at all sorts of things.
Growing *requires* failure.

The alternative is to become moldy,
and, sometimes, we do get a little moldy.

So what!?
Scrape it off; try something else.
Just don't give up on the Journey.

Simply trying to stay on the Path —
is itself the Path.
Do the next good thing on your list and know that it is right,
because you are right where you are supposed to be.

Intention:
Do I understand that the Path
is simply continually trying?

## 142. Give Yourself Grace

You don't suck

Stop telling yourself that you suck.
Would you wish that on anyone else in your life?
Extend the same Grace to yourself that you extend to others.

Believe in taking care of yourself.
This is the definition of self-care.
It begins with that internal monologue.
Don't excessively punish yourself.
That is simply abusive,
and the world is hard enough
without you riding yourself down.

If you start in on yourself, stop the habit.
Replace it with something positive.
Do this every single time,
even when you want to double down on self-abuse — don't.

Create a mantra that reminds you
to love yourself first and foremost.
Believing in yourself begins with knowing
you can make a mistake,
and become a better person
as a result of that mistake.

Intention:
Do I offer myself Grace when I make a mistake?

## 143. You Are Perfect

So Stop Worrying so much.

You are Perfectly where you need to be,

Whatever whackado,
negative thing you tell yourself
must be shut down.

The world is busy enough riding us down,
we can't be an accomplice to that nonsense.
We need to learn how to build ourselves up
so we can keep moving forward.
We can't depend on other people to do that for us.
That is exhausting for you and for them.

Be your own advocate.
Be your best advocate.

Intention:
Do I have tools that combat self-sabotage?

# Your Body Is Perfect

## 144. Love the Mirror

*"I've been looking at myself in the mirror,*
*saying don't leave me now, don't leave me now."*
*- MUNA*

No matter what.
No matter what shape you are in.
No matter what hideous words come to mind.
If you are unhealthy, you can address that.
But, you must love yourself enough to do that.

Look in the Mirror,
and love that person on the Journey.
Love them right on down the Path.
Look at them in all their fabulousness,
and tell them that they are deserving of health and happiness.

If this kind of talk is making you feel uncomfortable,
well, good news — it's a mirror.
No one ever needs to know what you are saying to it.
Just look at yourself with enough love
to become your own number one fan.

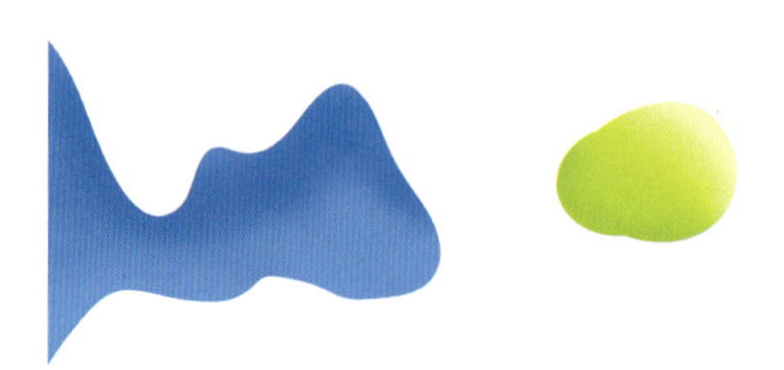

Intention:
What do I see when I look at myself?
Can I make that a bit more positive?

## 145. Stay Present

*Where else would I be?*

"What if" and "if only I would have" are virtual hells.
Daydreaming, on occasion, is fine,
but living in regret of the past,
or anxious of the future
is so completely self-sabotaging.
Stay in the moment.

If you want to change your life,
you can work on a plan.
*Use your Present to construct your Future.*
Nothing stands in your way except for your own mind.

Changing how we mentally treat ourselves is an exercise,
and, like exercise, we can build those muscles to be healthy.
Practice bringing your mind
to a sound, positive, present space
whenever it wants to wander toward
the unknown, hysterical, lands of worry and regret.

Then, forgive yourself for not being perfect.

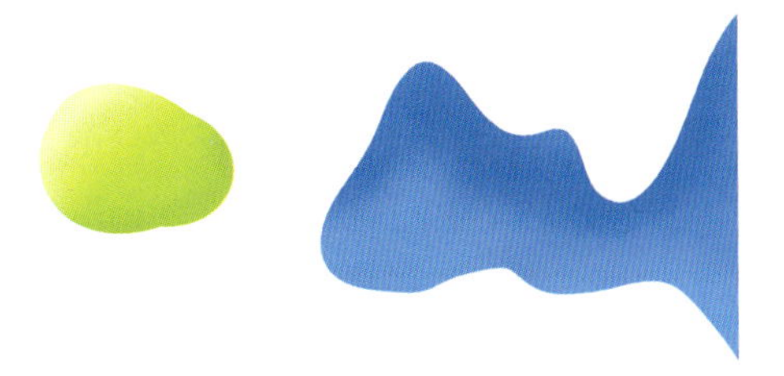

Intention:
Do I waste energy on worry?
Can I train myself to stay present?

## 146. Understand the Mystery of Journeying

Alexa - play "Building a Mystery" by Sarah McLachlan.

We don't know everything,
and that is perfectly okay.
Fear is *never* the answer.

The Mystery is what can replace fear.
Get excited about the Mysteries in life.
When you think of something that gives you fear,
don't give over to it.
Replace it with something deeper.
Something greater.

You don't have to walk around all dewy eyed and idiotic
to have this be a part of your day.
Just acknowledge the greatness of the universe.

Look at NASA photos!
They will show you the wonders of the universe.
Experience the amazing mystery of nature.
Pray to God. Pray to someone else's God.
Meditate and be amazed at the unknown of the mind.

It doesn't matter how you get there, just open up and let it in.
Whatever it is! It is your Mystery and you get to define it.

Intention:
Can I replace fear with something greater?
Can I allow for mystery?

# 147. Mental Health And Food Are Related

*Cakes are healthy too, you just eat a small slice.*
*~ Mary Berry*

Okay, we are never perfect at any of this.
There is no shame in reminding ourselves
that our mental health depends greatly
on the mind-body-soul connection.
You may hear this as shame,
but we need to try to reverse that kind of thinking.
Talking about food, faith, or exercise isn't shameful.
We want to normalize a healthy conversation
about this stuff, and not a harping one.
No one here is saying you have to be a size 4,
or have perfect muscles, or be anything along any of those lines.

What we *are* saying is that it is important to notice
the connection between our bodies and the way we feel.
For example: when we have the flu,
it is not easy to connect to anything on a spiritual level.
The same goes for when we eat, or drink, or smoke crap.
Take note of how you feel each day
in relation to what you put in your body.
Notice related emotional and physical trends.
How do you feel the next morning?
Really get to know how they all affect each other.

There is no weight or measurements going on in this.
That isn't what this is about.
This is an exercise in seeing how what we eat and drink
affects our anxiety and fear.

Intention:
Do I close myself off to seeing a relationship
between my mind and body because of shame or denial?

# 148. Try Positivity

Or at the very least
try to not be a bitch.

We all have days where we feel evil on the inside;
this is not the fault of everyone else around us.
On those days, we can dive into our ever-growing toolbox,
and try breathing our way through it.

Maybe you can take it a step further.
A little transparency and positivity outward,
even if you don't feel it,
can help you cope with those negative feelings.

This is important for two reasons.
One, it isn't everyone else's fault that you are feeling bitchy.
You damage relationships
when you take negativity out on others.

Two, a little transparency and positivity
about the way you are feeling
can soften your emotions.

Really, just say out loud,
"God, I'm feeling bitchy today."
You will feel less bitchy!
And, you probably won't shank anyone in the process.

Intention:
Do I bury my negativity?
Can I let those emotions out
instead of having them come out sideways?

# 149. Tell That Bitch To Shut Up About Your Body

Seriously.

Stop living in a head that hates you!
That hair, that fat, that — ugh… shut up!

You are *awesome* and you are on a Path,
so, tell that bitch to listen up!
You are doing one little thing at a time,
and they can just *get in line.*

The only purpose they serve is to make you feel overwhelmed,
and incapable of accomplishing anything.
That is ridiculous. There is no timeline here!
They don't get to say you are a failure.
You aren't done!
Shut her up.

Do one little thing. That is all.
Do one little thing and shut her up.
You do not need to do and be everything right this minute.
You are on a Journey.
She needs to join you there.

Intention:
Do I let my head overwhelm me
to the point that I am paralyzed?
Do I know that I don't have to do everything right now?

# 150. Comparison Is the Devil

A SOCIAL MEDIA LAMENT.

How can we justify comparing ourselves
to someone who is so completely different than us?
Here's a better plan:
build yourself up to be the person you want to be,
regardless of anyone else or their Path.

Others are not the problem.
Our own lack of self-esteem is.
Instead of tearing someone else down,
try saying "Good for them".

Becoming the person we want to be is on us.
Some of us will never be dainty.
Some of us will never be 5'10.

It is all in recognizing what we bring to the table.
Instead of looking at what someone else is,
look at what you are, and what you want to be.
No one gets to take that away from you.
Digging deep and spending time defining
what you like about yourself will create an inner beauty
and strength that will shine through.

Celebrate others instead of comparing yourself.
You both have so much to offer.

Intention:
How do you see yourself? Do you know your strengths?
Dig deep and see what you love about yourself.

# 151. Celebrate Diversity

## In Everything!

Seriously, everything.
Not just because it is a good thing to do.
Being afraid of things that are different from us
leads us down a road that, eventually,
will make us hate something about ourselves.
None of us are made from cookie cutter patterns.
If we have something about ourselves that is a little different,
we tend to look at it with shame.
We don't know how to celebrate our own diversity.
If we make a habit of learning about peoples and cultures
that are really different than us, we can react
to things with less fear.
Also, we can react to ourselves with less fear.
It's a win-win.

Intention:
Do I react with fear to things different than me?
Can I embrace diversity, truly?

## 152. See The Splendor In Everyone

GW - even Greg?
- they chew with their mouth open.

It isn't easy to constantly see the best in everyone.
The rule in life is: get up and try.
Fail by 11AM. Try again.

Sometimes we don't like people
because we fear we are similar.
Sometimes we don't like people
because we fear they are different.
Sometimes we don't like people
because we think we are better than they are.
Sometimes we don't like people
because we think they are better than us.
Sometimes we just feel evil on the inside.

Try a little harder to see beauty in the people around you.
It's not their fault they don't live up to your expectations.
You put those expectations on them in the first place,
and this only eats away at your soul;
it doesn't do anything to help them.

Give yourself *and* them a break.
Look at people with a little more love in your heart.
Surprisingly, it is so much easier to see the world this way.

Intention:
Can I cut the world a little slack?
Do I see how this only helps me?

# 153. Eat Too Much; Eat Too Little

– Make up your
damn mind –

What is your specific relationship with food?
We are living in an industrial food society,
and we all have some issues in this area.

Do you have tight control over every morsel,
or are you a binge eater? Somewhere in the middle?

Even that gal who works out, eats healthy,
and seems like she has never struggled
a day in her life — has issues with food.
She is at a different place in her Journey,
sure, but she knows the struggle.

On this Journey, we are beginning
to identify all sorts of issues,
and this is often a big one.

Start by letting go of a food habit that defines you,
even if it's only for one day.

What are your food habits?
Can you identify them?
How do they control your life?
How do they define you?

Intention:
How is my relationship with food?
Do I recognize my habits?

## 154. Know How to Forgive Yourself

*It's actually kind of annoying if you don't.*

Self-torture is self-obsession.
Read that again.

You cannot learn a damn thing
if you are busy wallowing in the muck
of your own swamp of self-loathing.
If you fall down at something,
you get back up. Right?
You also learn.

Learning from the fall is a vital part of moving forward.
When you fall, instead of self-torture,
focus on what you can do differently.
Look at the process clinically instead of emotionally.
If we separate the emotional response,
we grow, we adapt.
Don't waste time on
self-loathing and self-obsession;
Get up and go!

This obviously takes some practice,
but this is self-care. This is self-love.
Self-care and self-love are the opposite of self-obsession
because they allow us to grow outwardly.
This is the Path!

Intention:
Do I know how to forgive my mistakes and move forward?
Do I see how this is self-care?

# 155. Know Everyone Is On A Journey

Yes– even Karen.

We talk about comparison,
celebrating others, positivity, and our own Journey.
We have so much opportunity to learn from others' Journeys!

It is easy to celebrate
That-Hot-Bitch-Who-Has-Everything's Journey.
It is hard to celebrate
That-Curmudgeon-Who-Is-Cruel-And-Oblivious.

Here's the deal, none of it really matters.
They (and you) are all just freaking
trying their best to get along.
It isn't our responsibility to fix people,
judge people, or control them.
Not just because that is the nice thing to do,
but because that is what keeps us sane.

So, yes, everyone is on a Journey,
but start with knowing you are a part of that equation.
You get priority seating in your head,
and they don't get to take up space there.
You are the only one that can allow them
to occupy your seating.
Place them properly on their own Journey,
and get on with becoming a more fabulous version of You.

Intention:
Do I let other people's Journeys control my thoughts?

## 156. Your Body Is Perfect

We aren't Perfect.
We are perfectly us.

None of us are Perfect, so, stop with the negativity.
Do we want more this or that with our bodies?
Sure, who doesn't;
but let's look at this with cold-hearted honesty.

We are on a Journey, and our bodies
are perfectly where they are supposed to be.
If we want to get healthier — that is great!
That's definitely part of the Journey,
but we won't get anywhere until we realize
that we are already freaking Perfect!

*Yes! Right now!*

Like all things with mental health,
there is an element of Faith we have to put in ourselves
that leads us down the Path we want to be on.
The Path is the thing, not being Perfect.
The Path is perfectly where we are supposed to be
at this very moment.

Your body is Perfect because it has led you here to this moment.
Your body is Perfect because it helps create all of You.
You are on this Journey,
and this Body contains the Mind and Soul
that springs you forward down the Path.
Don't hate the body that has brought you here.
Celebrate it,
and move forward.

Intention:
Do I understand how my body is a beautiful part of me?

# Take The Risk

## 157. Let Go Of The Crap

*And— there is a lot of crap.*

Right now,
is there something in your life you are holding on to?
Some resentment, some regret, some moment?

By holding on to the Crap,
you help it to define you.
Don't do that!

You don't need Crap in your life defining you.
You need: sunlight, flowers, and happiness —
not your boss berating you, or the endless errors of your parents.
They are not what gets to hang out in your precious mind.
Only you can let them stay there.
Hire an exorcism expert if you must,
but get rid of them!
They are only there to torment you.

By holding on to the Crap,
you let it take root.
You have too much going on
to let these moments waste precious time in your soul.
If the crap is serious, see a therapist.
The important thing is to begin to
release the Crap,
and feel that weight lift off your shoulders.

Intention:
Do I hold onto things that hurt me?

# 158. Look Forward With Faith

Getting Mushy again?

No, not really.
Okay, maybe a little.

But listen,
you can look ahead in your life,
and decide where you want to be in a few years.
You can look past the moment you are in,
and make decisions about what you want to do next.
Nothing says you have to know
how that is all going to turn out.
If you don't try, however, you will never know.

If you don't plan a little, you can't make things happen.
So have a little Faith in the future.
Dream with a purpose. Make that dream a plan.
Then move forward.

If we want something to happen,
we have to take that leap of Faith.
Only fear stops us from moving toward that dream.
Fear is the opposite of Faith.
So have faith!

Intention:
Am I afraid to dream?

# 159. Meditate On Change

*"Time may Change me, but I can't trace time"*
*~ David Bowie*

"Change is the one constant in life" —
Some ancient Greek guy named Hericlitus said that.
Probably, someone said it before him.
Bowie sang about it.

The sooner you realize that all life is Change,
the easier it is to move forward.
Inevitably it leads to better things.
If it doesn't, it is only because
you haven't changed out of that place yet.

Sometimes we really struggle with this,
But it is in the changing that we grow, learn, and Become.

Look at what Change has brought you.
Look at what Not Changing has brought you.
Root deep, and sink into the idea of change.
It can be exciting if you let it.

Intention:
Do I fear Change?

# 160. Fortify Yourself With Self-Love

Self love is not
Self obsession.

Take care of yourself so you have the strength
and foundation to become the person you want to be.
Remember, only *you* know what is going on inside your head. No
one else is going to do it for you.

This is going back to school.
This is learning how to fence.
This is opening that Etsy shop.
This is finally leaving that asshole.

This is seeing down the line,
and knowing that you are worth it,
knowing that the better you are,
the better able you are to serve others.

This is the opposite of self-obsessive suffering.
In fact, this combats that kind of thinking.
If you fortify yourself with true self love,
you no longer need to suffer.
You don't depend on others to serve your needs.
You have created a foundation that makes you stronger.
You have decided to root for You.

Intention:
Do I understand what self-love is?
Do I know how to practice this in my life?

## 161. Investigate People You Admire

Commence the Google Search!

We are in the wonderous age of the internet,
and you can investigate all roads.

Do you want to learn something,
become something, do something, create something?
Look around; find someone who has already done it well.
Find out how they did it.
Investigate all the Paths and details.
Use someone else's experiences.
You don't need to reinvent the wheel.
You can copy their Path.
Imitation is the most sincere form of flattery.
Inevitably it will be your own unique path.
(Unless you plagiarize; we are not recommending that.)

We are recommending that you look around
at people you admire, and see how it is they became Them.
Maybe this includes the way they go through their day.
Maybe you just want to investigate their serenity.
Don't waste the resources around you!

Intention:
What do you admire in the people around you?
Can you see yourself on that Path?

# 162. Don't Do Jealousy

*"God help you if you are a phoenix and you dare to rise up from the ash.*
*A thousand eyes will smolder with jealousy*
*while you were just flying past"*
*~ Ani DiFranco*

There is nothing good for the receiver *or* the holder of Jealousy.
It destroys the soul faster than greed.
It ruins relationships. It destroys self-esteem.
It is the bane of high school locker rooms,
and the vestiges of that creep into our daily lives as adults.

Don't do it. Just don't.
Don't give credence to anyone who throws shade.
Escort those feelings right out of your heart,
and replace them with celebration.
Celebrate people's success.
Even the assholes.
It's not your job to fix them.
It's not your job to be an asshole back.
Screw that. Let them fly!

And while you are busy watching them fly,
get out your own broom, and fly your own path.
There is room here for all of us.

Intention:
Do I let Jealousy eat at my soul?

# 163. Ask Advice

*"Dear Abby, Dear Abby my feet are too long."*
*~ John Prine*

There is a long history in the world
of "decision by committee" prevailing.

President Kennedy utilized a multi-tiered committee
to prevent nuclear war in the Cuban Missle Crisis.
Israeli's Tenth Man concept is based on the idea
that if everyone agrees, someone should play devil's advocate.

The committee in our head
can't always be trusted; ask for help.
Ask people you respect what they think.
Surround yourself with people
who will question and challenge you.
Know that they are there to be supportive.
Make sure your gut is really your gut,
and not just blatant fear or ego.
If we all work together toward healthy goals,
we all benefit.

Intention:
Do I know how to ask for advice?
Can I use people I admire to help me make good choices?

# 164. Self-Evaluate

*That doesn't mean you need to tear yourself a new one.*

Evaluation is how we improve. Learn this skill.
It requires active participation, endless self-love, and patience.
It will allow you to move forward on your Path.
Don't hyper obsess about pointless minutiae
to compensate for what you know you need to work on.
Self-hatred is crafty that way.
It will want to hide in your brain,
wrapping itself up in camouflage,
so that you don't focus on it.

Evaluate the big moments in your life that, when stripped down,
we know inhibit us from becoming truly us.
Good news! You don't have to live in self-hatred anymore,
because we are all moving through these moments.
You are only required to acknowledge them,
and start down that Path.

This change does not happen overnight; that doesn't matter.
When you self-evaluate and really see yourself,
the Path is obvious.
Pain is a part of life,
and sometimes we have to move through that.

The point is,
you cannot get past something without moving through it.

Start with being honest with yourself.

Intention:
Do I look at myself honestly?
Do I know what I need to focus on?

## 165. Love your Quirks

Every single one of them.

Are you chatty, quiet, intellectual, dreamy,
forgetful, super organized?
Do you like chick flicks, or science fiction, or history?
Do you like obscure documentaries?
Do you get too excited about cats?
Do you have passion for civil rights?
Do fairies and witches strike at your core?
Does def poetry music out of Chicago turn your fancy?
Do you obsess over cooking shows?

Own it!

Let yourself be You.
The only person telling you that you can't be You… is You.
Own who you are; let those quirks bring you joy;
you can be a light for someone else to see.

Just because you aren't surrounded by people
who find Americana music to be a gift from God,
doesn't mean anyone else is wrong.
There is enough dissent out there already.
Maybe someone else will see your passion, and want to join in.
Maybe not, but you definitely won't drive
anyone away with this attitude.
Own your stuff and shine with it!

Intention:
Do I celebrate the unique things about myself?
Do I let them shine through me in a positive way?

# 166. Feel Uncomfortable

*No.*

You can separate yourself from uncomfortable moments
if you truly believe that learning is power.
When that uncomfortable feeling comes up,
focus hard on what you are learning from the situation
rather than how to run away from it.
Make that feeling become a trigger for learning.

Or maybe, just laugh at yourself.
Humiliation is self-sabotage,
and only we can allow this to happen.
Only we can allow for those emotions.
We are not made of circuits that feel no emotion.
Yes, sometimes we feel horrible about ourselves.
As with all things, this is an exercise, a tool for improvement.

Dig deep, and try to see the next
uncomfortable moment as a springboard.
What do you have to lose?

Intention:
Do I have the courage to move through discomfort to learning?

## 167. Account Your Present Situation

*"I'm sitting here alone in my room,*
*I got nothing to do but keep my mind off you."*
*~ Madeline Jaina*

What are you doing?
What do you want to do?
What is standing in your way?
What are the best choices for you if no one else mattered?

Start there. That is self-care.
Allow yourself to say out loud what it is you need.
Too often, we put the needs of others before us
to the point that we barely know who we are anymore.

What is your favorite color,
what is your favorite food,
who are you, really?

Checking in and accounting for where you are at present
will help you identify what it is you need.
What is it that you are blocking?
What is it that you want to do?

Intention:
Can I take honest stock of who I am, and where I am ?

# 168. Dig Deep

*We talking tulip bulb deep, or full-on dinosaur bones?*

Dude, full-on dinosaur bones!
We can't become the Amazon warrior or ass-kicking Pixie
we want to be if we aren't real with ourselves.
Authenticity will not fail you.

First, before you can be truly authentic
you must know who you are.
This is shockingly difficult for most of us.
We think we know who we are.
Or we dabble in knowing,
but run away when the answers are hard.

Dig deep for the good, the ugly, and the bad.
There is no judgement. There is only progress.
A therapist is always a good choice;
you can start with a journal,
or a group. You can find one for all sorts of issues
from drugs, to eating, to sex.
All these groups exist on the internet to help you.
Transparency is the ticket to find authenticity.
Dig deep and let it all out.
This is the Path.

Intention:
Can I break down the fear of getting to know myself truly?

## 169. Take The Risk

*"It's a dangerous business, Frodo, going out your door."*
*- Bilbo Baggins, Lord Of The Rings*

Every wonderful moment is precipitated by a Risk.
Your sheer existence required all sorts of Risks —
from conception to the delivery room.

In X amount of time,
you could be much further down your Path,
or you can stay here and wonder
if you should have done something.

You have tools.
You have unlimited time despite that voice in your head.
You have passion and dreams.
You can make a plan.

Take a Risk.
Fall, get up and take another Risk.
Win! Move forward, Fall. Get up. Fall again.
Get up. Fall again. Get up. Win. Win. Win. Fall.

Look back, and see what an amazing Journey
you have been on because you decided to take that Risk.

We don't carelessly throw everything out the window.
We study, plan, then do!
This is the basis of a successful project —
Why shouldn't it be the basis of a successful life?

Intention:
Can I see how important it is to take Risks?

# Develop Grit

## 170. Be A Little Hard On Yourself

*The hard work definitely paid off and hard work always does.*
*~Gabby Douglas*

Yes, we want to feel strong and empowered.
Getting to that point also requires us to be Accountable.
No one can do that for you, except You.
Along with all this discussion of self-empowerment
must come a real talk about holding yourself
to certain standards.

The thing is, we can't look back at a Journey
if all we have done is conceptualize it.

We have to put one foot in front of the other,
and actually do things that move us
to the state of being we want to live in.
If every day you are taking the mulligan,
and never the risk… there is no going forward.
We also can't spiral into a shame fest at each fall.
Find a balance instead.
Journal, goal set, and keep getting back up and trying again.
You can't fail this way;
you can only move forward.

Intention:
Do I love myself enough

# 171. Understand Boundaries

*"Boundary: something that fixes or indicates a limit or extent."*
*- Merriam Webster*

We cannot be everything to everyone.
God knows some of us try.

We also can't allow our own minds
to be the invasion force that leads us to crazy town.
That is also in our genetic make-up.

Boundaries are essentially
understanding what we need
in order to protect ourselves from ourselves.
How do we learn to say no?
How do we stop listening to that hate-fest in our head?
How do we create boundaries against our own self-sabotage?

Start by recognizing what we are doing to ourselves.
If we don't recognize we are doing it, we can't change it.

Once we start to identify
what we do to ourselves,
we can create boundaries.
We can practice saying no.
We can reach out to others for help.
We can create a safe zone around ourselves
so that we can grow.

Intention:
What do I do to myself to prevent growth?
Do I see where I lack boundaries?

# 172. Let The Sun Shine In

Back to the Groovy Shit!

Come on!
Sometimes we just have to decide to smile.
This is an exercise.
We can focus on the negativity in life,
or we can look around and be amazed.

Who do you want to sit next to at lunch?
Debbie Downer or Susie Sunshine?
Well, probably neither…
but the people who are genuine in their happiness
are the ones who are working at it daily.

We can work at identifying our own pessimism.
We can work at not adding to its fire.
We can immediately stop our line of thinking,
and say the opposite in our head.
This isn't crazy. This is truth.
The most influential speaker in *our* world is Us.
If we can learn to change the dialogue, we can shine.

Intention:
Do I see how my own negativity affects my own happiness?

# 173. Don't Let Denial Sneak In

*"I could deny it if I liked. I could deny anything if I liked"*
*- Oscar Wilde*

Because we can be so unbelievably hard on ourselves,
we use Denial regularly as a coping mechanism. Drop it.
You are on a Path now that only sees you as moving.
Not good or bad, just moving forward.

What are the things you know hold you back?
What are the things you do that you know are unhealthy?
What are the things you have to talk yourself into believing?

Start there.
If you have to *make* yourself believe it… you may be in Denial.
If it is an addiction with drugs, including alcohol,
get help now. No discussion.

If you are looking at a myriad of other problems, break it down.
Here is something simple: smoking is bad for you.
Eventually it will lead to serious respiratory problems.
Do you have to quit today? Nope.
But, know that you are too smart to stay in Denial forever.
The same goes for a million of other things,
like sugar, obesity, pills, sex, social media, gaming, etcetera!
There is no shame, just recognition.
This way, when you do decide to change,
you don't have to fight the Denial first.
It is a part of you and at some point,
on your Path, you will address it.

Intention:
Do I deny that there are things in my life
I need to work on in order to protect my self-esteem?
Can I recognize them without tearing myself apart?

## 174. Let Someone Know You

What kind of "knowing" are we talking about here?

The kind where you are flat-out honest about:
who you are on the inside, your greatest fears,
your self-perception, your dreams — everything.

Does that sound terrifying?
Good, then you are on the right track.
If you don't have someone that knows you like this,
a therapist is in order.

This business of hiding who we are from the world
is part of what prevents us
from being the person we want to be.

It is more than likely that you are doing one of two things.
One, you are likely twisting reality in your head.
Saying what you are thinking out loud
allows someone else to give you a perspective adjustment.
Two, you are riding yourself down for things that are irrelevant.
Not all the time, of course,
but when we get in that dark place, these things are going on.

Don't keep it in.
Call in your committee of friends, and be honest.
Call a therapist. Check in with your partner.
Tell the truth in your head to someone.

Intention:
Can I be truly honest about who I am?

## 175. Compare Yourself To YOU

She's Soooo –

Scenario:
Fifteen years ago, you are working at a job. You are 40 pounds overweight, and feel exhausted all the time. You decide to start running one to three miles. You don't have time to do more because of the kids. You are trudging along, but have decided you might be worth investing in.

Five years later, you are running in an occasional race, and it keeps you moving. Work is not a priority, but you are saying yes to professional opportunities. You eat sugar like it's your holy food, and you drink ½ bottle (at least) of wine almost every night. You are 20 pounds over your healthy weight, but you feel so much better. You are proud of yourself for what you have accomplished.

Five years later, the kids are driving. You have taken a ton of responsibility at work that you enjoy. You have conquered a couple of marathons, but you mostly just exercise now for mental health because it has become a regular part of your life. You found Yoga and meditation. You only drink when you are out, and you have lost 10 more pounds. You are proud of every aspect of your life. You are still obsessed with sugar, but you basically feel like, "Who gives a shit!" You open a roadside bakery.

Intention:
Compare this woman to the woman 15 years ago.
That is all. Nothing. Else. Matters.

## 176. You Are The Best

### Because Nothing Else Matters.

Continuing on with the "Don't Compare" theme.
You are the best, because you are invested in You.
It doesn't matter where You are in life,
You are the Best right this minute, for this minute.
Then, You get better, and You are also the Best then.

Since You aren't comparing yourself to anyone but You,
You get to always be on top.
It is such a relief to know
that you don't have to beat anyone else at anything.
You are it.

As You move along the Path,
You get to be amazed at everything
that You are improving in your life — both big and small.

This is the beauty of seeing the big picture.
You don't have to do it all right now.
You are already the Best!

Intention:
Do I appreciate all that I am right at this very moment?

# 177. Take The Time

*"Rome wasn't built in a day."*
*~ Some French Poet circa 1190*

It is amazing to realize
that something that was written by a poet,
almost a millennia ago, is relevant today.
That is some divine wisdom, people!

You can't have it all tomorrow.
You *can* start building it, though.
You can get outside of your head,
and make a plan.

Sometimes we struggle
with seeing our own part in our Plan.
We struggle with the idea
that we are somehow responsible for it.
We don't understand
that it takes time and commitment to make change happen.
We don't see that we can either:
start down the road, or not start down the road.

In choosing to not start, we are choosing to not build.
No one is going to build your Rome except you.
Do just a little bit every day to make that happen.
Then, you get to look back and see how far you've come.

Intention:
Do I allow myself time to grow,
or do I expect immediate change?

## 178. Put In The Effort

Rome was built by slaves
so—that isn't an option

This is the actual hard part.
We fill our days with tasks,
and see our time as committed and exhausted.

This is a mental game.
You don't have to do it all at one time.
But really, look at everything.
Something can give.
Maybe it's that bottle (eh hem, ½ bottle) of wine.
Give that up, and you get energy and time!
Maybe it's the fact that your kids
don't need you every second of the day.
In fact, that is not always the best thing for them.
(See Harvard longitudinal study on working mothers).
Maybe it's the endless tasks you have assigned to yourself.

Cut a moment out of your day for some self-care.
Put the effort into what you want to do,
or Be, or accomplish.
Understand that this self-care
is dreadfully important over time.
Do what you know you need to do,
and investigate how to do the rest.

If you change nothing, nothing changes.
Put in some effort.

Intention:
Do I realize that effort
toward myself is the actual definition of self-care?

# 179. See The Changes

*"If you don't like something change it.*
*If you can't change it, change your attitude."*
*~ Maya Angelou*

We often feel overwhelmed,
and we don't see the Changes we have made.
Don't quit!

Look at the Journey; see the Changes.
It is easy to ignore little Changes
as if they are of no consequence.

All change happens over time.
If a flower quit growing because it was frustrated
with how freaking long it took,
this would be a much uglier planet.

Similarly, we have zero control over other people's Journeys.

Zero.

Take a page out of my favorite, phenomenal, deep-voiced
poet/author Maya, and change your attitude.
Your Journey is for you alone.
See the changes you have made,
and let others have their own Path.

Intention:
Am I willing to see the positive changes in my life?
Do I focus only on the things I can control?

## 180. Let Failure Guide You

Not Define You.

This is beginning to feel like a mantra,
but falling down is a precursor to getting up.

Living in misery is a choice.
Clinical depression is real and needs treatment,
but suffering is different.
We can root down in our suffering
like a comfy little onesie that will contain us for life.
It is a sick place to be.
Most of us don't even recognize when we are rooting.
It is comfortable to surround ourselves with that pain.
But it is a true sickness.

Here it is:
Bad things happen.
We can let them define us,
or we can move through them
and become better because of them.

Our misery isn't because of our tragic past —
it is a result of not moving through the pain.
Our misery isn't because of the people in our lives —
it is because we don't deal with our own responses.
Failure, pain, and trauma are all things that we go through.
Let them guide you to a better place, not define you.

Intention:
Do I see myself as empowered?

# 181. Know You Are Worth It

Is this a L'Oreal Ad?

Damn right it is.

In 1973, Ilon Specht was the first woman
to write an ad campaign for L'Oreal,
An ad written by a woman for women.
At the age of 23, she came up with the catch phrase

*"Because you're worth it".*

Almost 50 years later, L'Oreal is still using it.
That is how much this ad campaign struck a chord.
Do we, sisters and others, not know our worth, or what?
These simple four words were enough
to become a permanent part of our lexicon
because someone, apparently, forgot
to include our worth along our developmental lines.
We keep forgiving them, and taking on the burden.
Not any more, my beautiful ones!
We are worth far more than dime-store mascara.
We are worth every ounce
of every bit of work, love, and support
we have doled out over the course of the many generations,
and it is time to mean it when we say,
"Because I'm worth it".

Intention:
Know your worth. Deny your shame.
Own your fierce and wonderful self.

# 182. Develop Grit

*Angela Lee Duckworth actually wrote a formula for this.*

For those of you that need the formula, check out her book. It's a great read. In short, you don't need to be perfect at anything. You don't need to be the best. You need to be resilient, creative, conscientious, and see the long game.

In a less academic sense, you need to fall down and get up. Be less deterred by the fall, and more intrigued with the lesson. Perfectionism will destroy dreams. Resilient responses, and creative solutions are what is needed to get through any trial. When you feel crushed by a moment, stop and look at what you are seeing. Can you add this to your toolbox? Can this be an impetus of change that will help you in the future?

Can you change your natural response to something from being mercurial to something more productive? Can you develop a little more grit, and little less drama?

That hot-headed, screaming lady, remember, is full of fear. The gritty lady is responding with direct problem-solving before anyone else even realizes a problem needs solved. Will we be the gritty lady in every situation? Of course not — we aren't Fairy-born magical creatures. We are human, but, with a little grit, we can sometimes feel like warriors.

Intention:
How gritty am I?
Can I see where I need to work on this?

# Pray

## 183. Cry

Feel all the feels

And know that is perfectly okay!

Sometimes we crush emotion to protect ourselves.
This leads to every kind of sideways behavior:
snappiness, mood altering choices
(like drinking or shutting out others),
and general anxiety and depression.

Instead, it may be easier to just feel the feels.

More importantly, be honest about your feelings.
Be honest with yourself.
Be honest with those around you.
Stop crushing what is really going on inside you
because you are afraid.

All that does is give those fears more power.
Then, we are back to the above list.

You're not weird.
You are scared, or sad, or just in need of a good cry.

The way to get in touch
is to take the risk
and say
how you really feel.

It's really okay.

Intention:
Do I know what I am feeling?
Can I allow myself to feel this?

# 184. Connect With Something Good

Like a cup of good tea
or Facetime c̄ a friend.

We are bad ass bitches. Sometimes in the daily fight to exist, we forget the importance of simple human kindness. This is good for everyone around us, right? Yes, and this is the kicker,
it is good for us.

Something about taking the time for kindness or goodness grows our own soul exponentially. This is not always easy. That evil pathological whack-a-doo who lives across the street is not on your Journey. She is likely confused, miserable and, sadly, completely self-unaware. By really trying to connect with goodness, you can let go more easily of the need to meet her with aggression or annoyance.

And that brings you peace.

You can't change w-a-d, but you can understand she is suffering, and by being more in touch with goodness you get to feel emotionally better yourself.

It is a win-win.

Intention:
Do I know how to connect with goodness?
Can I put that out in my world?

# 185. Believe In Something

I believe in this roll of tape.

We don't recommend a roll of tape, but if that is going to get you to connect with something greater, fine. The point is, we want to understand that there are things in the universe that are beyond our capacity. If you are straight up atheist, then understand why this is so important. Humility gives us the gift of a truly open mind, and the potential to dig for something deeper. Understanding we aren't the final say in everything allows us to access parts of our mind that heal the ugly bits in our past.

The trick is, you have to be open to the idea that this is possible. If you are truly a lover of science, this is easy because the mind is an amazing thing. Faith is the easiest way to do this. And let's be honest, it is all the same thing if you look at it as understanding and respecting that there are things we don't understand.

This is your Journey, and your Path alone. Spend some time with this concept. If you already have a faithful practice, spend some time understanding how that should lead you to humility (not superiority). We are all trying to figure out life; a little Faith and humility opens us up to all possibilities — including healing.

Intention:
Do I understand how Faith or Belief can open my mind?

## 186. Remember What Makes You Laugh

I don't have time for this nonsense—
I've got too much on my to-do list—

None of us have time
to take care of something simple, like remembering to Laugh.

We fill up our days with too many tasks and fail at half of them.
We get frustrated and overwhelmed.
When did we last belly Laugh?
When will we allow ourselves to have fun?
What is so damn important?

Within all of the hububaloo,
have you taken a minute to truly enjoy yourself?
If we don't, what is the actual point of all of this?
Take a minute to look at your life, and understand
the things that bring you joy.
Understand what makes you Laugh.
If this is a struggle, it is long overdue.

Intention:
What makes me Laugh? What brings me joy?

## 187. Laugh With Someone

Take the Show on the Road.

Simply share the Joy.

Just like hate and vitriol spread like a virus,
so do laughter and Joy.
Have you ever laughed at something
because the person sharing it is laughing so hard?
You can't help but laugh with them.

This is spreading Joy.

Take earnest moments to find Joy with another person.
Try to do this in person—although a good text or email
can also bring about the same sensation.
That connection through laughter can sometimes mean more in a
relationship than hours of conversation.
We are not automatons that need to behave perfectly
every second of the day.
If someone is a bit of a goof,
draw on that energy and see how fun life can be.

Intention:
Do I share in others Joy?

# 188. Allow Your Mind To Change

We aren't Gods.

The surest way to close your mind, like a steel trap, is to believe there is only one way to do something. One way to see the world. One way to think. One way to believe. If you knew what was best for everyone, you would be a God. If you think it is your job to manage those that don't think the same way you do, then you are likely exhausted with that responsibility… because we aren't God. Isn't it hard enough trying to manage our own lives without getting so concerned about how to make everyone else see things exactly as we do? And if we are busy trying to do that, we miss all the learning opportunities we could have through investigating people who think differently. If you are reading this and thinking to yourself, "Those (insert group you don't like here) need to read this."

Stop.

We cannot expect people to hear us,
when we don't recognize that we aren't hearing them.

Breathe in, breathe out.
Hear differences.
Be okay.

Intention:
Am I truly, really truly, open to other's beliefs?
Can I work towards opening my mind?

## 189. Remember Those Before You

Build on the lessons of the ladies before you.

Who are you? What do you like to do? What is important to you? At some point in history somebody likely paved a way for you to get here. If you are a woman in western society, someone starved themselves, went to prison, and did decades of organizing to get you the most basic and fundamental rights, like voting or owning property. If you are anywhere on any spectrum of people that have had a Journey to get to a place in society that is improving over the last iteration (marginal as that may be), many people worked to get you there.

We all stand on the backs of people who worked to move us ever forward. When you feel overwhelmed and exhausted and lacking any kind of grit, remembering the Journey of those before us can help bring us strength.

If Lucy Burns can starve herself and go to prison in the quest to get women the right to vote, we can get through the shift with that jerk faced coworker and live to fight another day. He can try to take your pleasant disposition, but he can't take your right to vote. A bad ass bitch secured that for you 100 years ago. You get to be a bad ass bitch because of her, and we can all learn from and celebrate the women that came before us in times of stress.

Intention:
Who's shoulders do I stand on?

## 190. Do Something Out Of Your Comfort Zone

Nude Sunbathing is out
of my comfort Zone—

Well, maybe, don't walk around naked.
No one is judging,
but no one is telling you to do that either.
This is a 'what can I do to move me forward in life'
kind of thing.
Go to a church,
go to a drum circle,
go to an informational meeting at a college,
go see music by yourself.

This list could get really lengthy,
because there are an unlimited
number of things to do in the world.
This is about stretching ourselves to become the person
we have always wanted to be.
Are we scared of something?
What is holding us back?
What do we have to do to move past that?

Start there.

Do the first thing that introduces
us to the Path we want to be on.
Then, follow your feet.

Intention:
Who do I want to become?
What can I do to start that process?

## 191. Break Up Your Routine

*How…?*

–Seriously – How?

The day in and day out of our lives can make us crazy.
Fear sometimes traps us into a routine
that can drive us into insanity from the sheer monotony of it.

Shake it up.
Put in for a day of sheer fun.
Allow yourself to be free for just one stretch of time.
Even if it is half a day, give yourself the gift of freedom.
If you think there is no way you can do this,
then you must schedule it into your life, like a hair appointment.

Turn your world topsy-turvey for a minute or two.
Care enough about yourself to allow
for this kind of break in your routine.

How to do that?
It simply starts with the decision to.

Intention:
Do I care enough about myself to break up my Routine?

## 192. Look At Your Daily Rituals

What Daily Rituals?

If you don't have daily rituals that ground you,
start there.
Right now you are reading a daily direction book,
so that is a daily ritual.
*Good!*
Do you have a way you start and end your day
that allows you just a moment of introspection?
Do you clean off your emotional table at the end of the day?
Do you wake up and take a moment
to set your mind toward something positive for the day?
These small, momentary, check ins
can become the habit of a lifetime.

This is self-accountability that propels us forward
toward the person we want to be.

When it feels stale, change it up.

Intention:
Do I have something that grounds me every day?

## 193. Be Willing To Be Better

We can't Be Perfect Every Damn day!

Don't try to be perfect every day. It is impossible.

The key is to be willing and open
to being a better person
... every day.
That way, when the opportunity strikes,
you have the right mind set.
You don't know everything.
You don't need to know everything.
You just need to be open to improvement.
You can hear and see Paths,
instead of wallowing in unworthy thoughts.
You can take advice, accept help, set limits and goals,
develop that grit and keep moving forward.
The actual goal is not the point.
The Journey is the point.
You are on a Path and you will improve.

Make sure that you are willing.

Don't fight it, be open to it.

Intention:
Do I have willingness and openness,
or am I fighting my own Path?

## 194. Tap Into The Magic

### Are we back to the 70s?

A little, maybe. What makes your heart swell?
What can you connect with that elevates you?
That is the thing that you must develop.
For a lot of people, it is a religious practice.
That is awesome, and super easy to investigate.
If your heart shuts down when you hear the word religion,
investigate something else.
This is ultimately the thing that will not ever let you down.
This is a practice or a faith that is there for you
when you are having those days that move you to a dark place.
You must develop a well of magic that you can dip into
when your world seems bleak.
For the scientific types,
think of this as an endorphin access point.
Find a practice that takes you outside of your own head
and allows you to transcend.

Intention:
What do I do to move me outside of myself?

# 195. Pray

*"Purity and sensitivity mean*
*that we receive a cosmic paycheck everyday."*
*-Light on Life, B.K.S. Iyengar*

You don't have to believe in anything.
Prayer is a tool.
I could go down a scientific pathway
that explains what is behind the science of faith,
but what a snoozer.
Who cares anyway?
Does it move me to a place that is happier and healthier?
Great! Let's do that! Light a candle if it helps.
Be grateful for the things you have. Ask how you can become
the example of what you want to be in the world.
Believe with every fiber of your being that this force
is only pure light and good.
That is critical.
Let go of your pain.
Give up the pain, anger, frustration and control issues.
Give everything up in prayer.
Give it away.
Ask for there to be space for peace in your soul
and focus on that.
A great open space that can be filled up with God,
or with peace, or with Spirit,
or with submicroscopic energy particles.
Whatever it is, practice developing a relationship
with something that can fill that space.
It takes practice, so just start.

Intention:
Do I know how to pray in a way that feels authentic to me?

# Recommit

## 196. Give Up

But I have to fight!!!

No. No, you sure don't.
For some of us this goes against
every fiber of our beings.
So, picture yourself in a river
swimming upstream and moving nowhere,
getting exhausted and forgetting
where you were trying to go in the first place.
Then picture yourself letting go,
floating with the current downstream.
You are guided by forces
that are greater than you to a big open pool.

Now you have rested, you have been guided and you are strong.
You swim to the shore and find the pot of gold you were
fighting for in the first place. You cannot find
what you are looking for if you are fighting against the flow.

Sometimes we have to put effort in, yes,
but that isn't the chaotic fight we are talking about.

Give up the chaos. Look for the quiet flow.
Let it guide you.

Intention:
Do I create chaos? Do I fight against help?

# 197. Look Around

*"You are one of the rare people who can separate your observation from your perception...you see what is, where most people see what they expect."*
*~ Tsitsi Dangarembga, Nervous Conditions*

The world does tend to pass us by while we are running around doing all of the things, but simple moments tie the days together by showing us how really amazing this world is.
From sunsets, to bird watching, to noticing how someone helps another person, we can see the beauty in the world. It does make the days a little more important, a little more palatable.
It also helps you commit to the bigger picture. If life is a series of beautiful days wrapped together, isn't that the point?
Why do we fret over all the details?

Look around. Something wonderful is happening right now.

Intention:
Do I spend time looking at the world around me?

## 198. Take Yourself Out Of The Center

This is layered → like an Onion.

Of course, we are the center of our world; we are the point of our world. There is nothing wrong with that. But everyone else is the center of their world. So, you can't be the center of their world also. Understanding this will help you understand that only you can fight for you.

Now, do we develop relationships that are partnerships where we get to rely on each other here and there? Yes, and that is great if you have someone who is there for you and to whom you give back support. In this way, you can develop a network, or a family that is supportive.

But each individual has their own life, and your job is to worry about yours. We aren't the center of the universe, just our world. So other people, places and things get to be their own thing. You just need to work on your own world. It tends to relieve a lot, if the world doesn't depend on us for everything. It's only our perception. And most likely, what is a big deal to you, isn't a big deal to everyone else.

Stop worrying about the world,
and get on with the business of taking care of you.

Intention:
Do I understand how to self-care, not self-obsess?

# 199. Address Regret

*"I regret those times when I have chosen the dark side."*
*~ Jessica Lange*

Look at where you are,
and be frank with yourself.
What do you Regret?
What do you wish you could have done differently?
What risks did you want to take?
Can you do any of these things now?
Can you address any pain you may have caused?
Can you forgive yourself?
Those are the choices,
and they can, and should, be addressed immediately.
Do the thing you Regret not doing.
Make amends for situations you Regret.
Forgive yourself for the things you can't change.
Don't go dark.
Try to do better.
That is all.

Intention:
What do I Regret? What can I do to address those?

## 200. Address Gut Anger

Do I get to PUNCH someone?

We are not big on violence.
With women this kind of anger sometimes
comes out sideways anyway.
Let's look at it.
What makes you apoplectic?
What makes your blood boil?
What starts you down an anger fest path?
Look at it.
What part of it is fear, ego or shame?
What, even in the worst situations,
makes you think that the anger that consumes you
is better for you than working through it?

Worst situation: Someone loses their child to violence.
The parent can spend their life in fury and fear.
Or, the parent can confront their fear
and their shame over not being able to protect their child
(understanding this is an irrational, but typical, response).
They can forgive the aggressor, and live free of that rage.
They don't have to do this for the situation, or the aggressor,
or even because they are the best Christians on the planet.
They do this because the gift to themselves
is that they get to let go of that all-consuming anger and fear.
There are some truly beautiful stories about this exact thing.

Intention:
What boils your blood?
What part of that anger can you own so that you can let it go?

## 201. Look At The Food Thing

It's been a minute, we must look at it again.

It isn't that we haven't talked about it,
it's that we have to keep talking about these things
so that we are super comfortable with them.
Food conversations that are healthy and positive
and constructive have to be a part of our lexicon
so that we can continue to move forward
with the triad of health.

How is that food and drink thing going?
There is no wrong answer.
There are not "good" or "bad" answers.
There is no answer that makes you "better".
The answer is just a reflection.
The answer is a way to look at the self with love and kindness.
With each time we address these things,
we get a little better at them.
We are never good or bad,
we are on the Journey.

Talk. Try one thing. Try another. Keep learning.

Intention:
Can I talk about food and drink choices without shame?
Do I know this is part of the Journey?

## 202. Look At The Moving Thing

*"As long as I can feel the beat, I don't need no money."*
*~ Sia*

The cheapest drug on the market are endorphins.
They are made when we get up and move our body around.
There is no replacement for physically moving the body.
There is no replacement for the grit and discipline
physical activity can sometimes take.
There is the bonus that moving helps with the food thing.
Do something today that gets you off your booty
and puts you in your happy chaps!
Do this not because you want to be skinny,
but because you want to be happy.
I mean, sometimes, while we are doing the movement thing,
we aren't so happy
(this is where the grit and discipline comes in).
But that is temporary!
Remember your grit!
Remember your path.
Remember to choose self-care.
Don't put thought or stress into it. Walk some stairs,
dance in the bathroom, take a walk. You can do this!

Intention:
What am I doing to put movement in my life?

## 203. Look At Relationships

So— how is it going?

How are we doing with the other people in our life?
Are they all idiots who deserve to die,
or are there one or two idiots?
Relationships are a barometer.
If everyone you know is a moron,
and all your relationships are with idiots,
then, so sorry, self-reflect and see that you are the problem.
Something is out of whack with you
and you need to start there—
in fact, all you can do is start there.

Do the therapy thing.
Do the journaling thing.
Look at what is going on with you
that makes the world so frustrating.
If there are only a few conflicts,
look at your part in the conflict.
What is it about those relationships that cause us
to be so angry or terrified or obsessed?
There is hidden guilt, shame, or pride in there.
Find out what sets us up to be angry.

Intention:
Are my relationships showing me something about myself?

## 204. Look At Behaviors

*"We are not going to change the whole world, but we can change ourselves and feel free as birds."*
*~ Sri S. Satchidananda, The Yoga Sutras*

The day we stop evaluating our own behavior
is the day that we give in to denial,
and when we give in to denial,
we fall off the Path.
We are not good or bad,
we are moving through.
We are getting better.
We are always in the process of this progress.
Stop seeing everything as good or bad.
When we look at how we are behaving,
we are evaluating how we are doing emotionally and spiritually.
Sometimes life is hard and we are lashing out.
Look at that. Look at triggers. Look at reactions.
What is under your control in your situation?
Change those things.
What can't you control?
Let that part go—even if this is hard.
Look at your reaction,
so you can recognize what needs changed.

Intention:
Do I see myself clearly?

# 205. Understand You Are Winning

Do I get a trophy?

Nope! No trophies.
But the concept behind, 'You are a winner',
is not wrong.
We focus so much on the failures in our head.
It can be paralyzing. It can lead us down a Path
of self-doubt that is no joke.
We may not even see it happening.
We start to ride our own selves down
to a level that leaves us paralyzed.
We are unable to move forward,
because we have convinced ourselves
that we aren't worth it.
We become so degraded that we are afraid to hope.
That damn bitch in your head is creating a maelstrom,
and we need to let her know the truth.
You are a freakin winner!

Maybe you haven't gotten the trophy yet,
but dammit, there are trophies coming!

Intention:
Do I see myself as a winner? Why the hell not?

# 206. Admit When You Need Help

I need help carrying this Big-Ass
Trophy Home.

We all get to a point in life, sometimes,
that requires us to reach out for some help.
Here is the deal, the longer you stay off the Path
pretending you don't need help,
the longer you live in misery.
It is really that simple.

ASK FOR HELP.
Stop fighting.
Get to the flow, and admit you need help.

Then accept the help,
and realize what great strength
comes from asking for what you need.
If you knew everything you wouldn't be here,
so listen and accept.
Or bash your head against the wall seven more times.
The Path will be waiting for you whenever you need it.

Intention:
Are there things I need help with?

# 207. Take Steps

*"Because dreams don't keep."*
*~ Amanda Shires*

We can't sit and wait for the world to come to us.
We have to do things.
Not all of them at once, not every single thing,
but like our girl (and iconic singer-songwriter),
Amanda Shires, points out,
dreams don't keep.
We have to feed them. We have to plan them.
We have to take the steps to make them real.
Once we know what we want to work on or achieve,
then we can take the steps.
Sometimes those steps suck.
Every job, dream, goal, self-improvement, or project
has aspects that suck.
(Remember that grit we talked about? That comes in
handy when we have to face challenging tasks.)
Do them.
Do all the steps to get to the place you want.
No one is going to magically hand you the script
and call you a movie star. This is folly.
Work for what you want,
then enjoy the results.
Then, do the next thing.
It just keeps getting better and easier.
The trick is to keep doing the things.

Intention:
Do I know what steps I need to take in order to move forward?

## 208. Recommit

YAASS – every. damn. day.

We have said it before.
Get up, fall down and recommit.
This is a Journey.
A big, beautiful, bold Journey
and you are carving out this Path that is yours,
and yours alone.
Get on it!
Have you lost motivation?
Are you feeling sad? Netflix to the rescue!
Then, get back up.
The key is not to stay down. You are allowed to fall.
You are allowed to learn!
That is what you are doing every single time things are hard.
You are learning how to be just that. Just be.
No more self-obsessing with all the criticism.
Stop beating yourself up as if you are some kind of
punishing God hell-bent on destroying yourself!
Get back up and recommit,
because you are a bad ass bitch
who deserves self-care.
Pick up your toolbox and get to work.

Intention:
Do I recommit to the Path? Do I allow myself to learn?

# Just Love People

## 209. See The Whole World

But you keep telling me
I'm not God—

It's a big, damn, difficult task seeing the whole world.
Having perspective helps with those big, self-reality checks.
It reaches 22 below zero in your town. Pretty damn cold.
And someone else says, 'Where's global warming now?'

Ha ha…

It's pretty funny when you are so cold your nose hairs freeze.
But global temperatures have been consistently warming
for thirty+ years. The ice caps are melting,
and the sea levels are rising.
It isn't called: our little corner of the world warming.
It is called: global warming.
Regardless of opinions,
we miss facts through perceptions of our world.
Our corner of the world seems like reality.
Now, if you are thinking that you aren't like that
because you think global warming is important,
you missed the point.
The story isn't about whether or not global warming
is important, but rather, how we tend to frame stories
from our own limited perspectives.
This story didn't offer an opinion about global warming.
It simply stated three measurable facts.
The framing of that was done by our own perspectives.
See the world outside of our own views.
It helps everyone.

Intention:
Can I try to see things from an outside perspective?
Can I see how my perspective and world experience
limit the way I see the world?

## 210. See Your Small Part In The World

*The good you do today*
*will often be forgotten, do good anyway.*
*~Mother Theresa*

When we are people who really feel the feels,
we tend to get overwhelmed with our causes.
Sometimes this is debilitating.
This kind of emotion is pretty useless for us
and pretty useless for our causes or beliefs or fears.
The first thing on the agenda with your
small part in the world is to create
the best freaking you that you possibly can.

Step one is self-care.

You are no good to anyone else,
until you are good to yourself.
When you are rocking the self-care thing
you can do the 'cause' thing well.
Even then, however,
your small part is unlikely to make a huge difference.
Do it anyway.
Do it because you will be better for it.
Do it and imagine what would happen
if everyone did self-care first,
then went out and did their small part.
Do it because we are all about the compassion revolution.

That is a world worth saving.

Intention:
Do I know that in order to be of value to others,
I must be of value to myself?

## 211. No Drama

*Now you're romanticizing some pain that's in your head.*
*~Joni Mitchell*

No drama is something so many people say,
right in the middle of creating it.
The life we have led has been full of different levels of drama.
Whether it is drama that swirls in our wake
or whether it is the drama we create in our heads.
We have all done it.
We fall into the maelstrom of chaos
that essentially sucks our soul out.
Some of us do it to ourselves.
Some of us create it in our environments.
Some of us, unwittingly, don't know how to exist
without these storms in our lives.
Almost like sitting with the quiet of life
is so boring to our souls
that we shake the shit out of things just to feel the pain.
This is not the path.
It takes a minute of walking down the path to realize
that deep joy is so worth the quiet moments
and the work that it takes to get there.

It doesn't happen perfectly,
so we all have moments of drama on the path.

What we can change now
is whether or not we feed them.
And how we react to them.

Intention:
How do I handle drama in my life?

## 212. Look At Your Bias

Its okay- We all have it.

Part of being able to see ourselves is being able to identify deep seated bias. Admitting that we have those things helps give ourselves the much needed perspective for self-evaluation.

Know what you don't know. Know what your experiences have done to shape your beliefs. Know you are not perfect, and know that is okay.

You are making your damn way like everyone else and you are allowed to have an opinion. Do one thing from now on: learn about your opinion outside of social media. This will cut down on the bias. Depend on documented sources. If you see something you don't like, double check the sources. If you see something that proves what you are already thinking, triple check the sources.

It is far more important to have accurate sources for what you do believe than to prove someone else wrong. If you feel strongly, find out if your feelings are justified. Get out of your primitive brain and into your frontal brain. Somebody has to evolve around here; it may as well be you!

Intention:
Do I blindly follow my gut emotions,
or do I take care to understand?

## 213. Connect With Someone Who Thinks Differently

I really don't see why -
they will likely annoy me.

Maybe a little — if you let them.
But this is where ultimate understanding
and inner peace can happen.
We can't hate everyone for their beliefs
and customs if we know they are
incredibly good people who love their children.
Hate is an easy reaction to fear and misunderstanding,
but it's so bad for you.
So bad for your gut.
So bad for all the good habits.
So bad for everyone.

This is why it is so important to take the time
and the effort to see our differences,
even when you think the way they believe
is full of trash or heresy.

This is when you can soften the edges of hate and fear.
You can learn, and maybe they can learn, too.

It is a straight up win for humanity.

Intention:
Can I listen to people who think differently than me?
Can I learn from them?

## 214. Listen To Different Music

*But her music is so...*

Our music taste often is closely tied to our biases.
When we spend time to understand other types of music,
we can see depth in all styles.
We can learn to appreciate things
that are outside of our wheelhouse.
We don't have to be a connoisseur of heavy thrash metal
who is also expected to love americana folk and indie-pop,
but we can learn to appreciate what the other offers.
Maybe lyrics, maybe the swell of the music,
maybe the beat, maybe the musicianship moves us.
This is an exercise in opening the mind to different things.
Music sparks passion in people. Find out why!

Intention:
Do I automatically discount people's choices in music?
Why do I do that?

## 215. Look At Art

*"Art is magic, magic is real, and*
*reality is stranger than dreams."*
*~ Pam Grossman*

The simplicity of looking at art
can open your mind in ways that invoke such peace.
The problem with our introduction to "art"
is it is so boring for so many of us.
The narrow definitions of art, placed by people
with too much time and money in our history,
do not expose us to all of the amazing, groovy, little things
out there that can blow our minds.
Next time you see a picture you think is pretty,
do a google deep dive on it.
See what art pops that you like.
See how that makes you feel.
Are you an art snob?
Open your heart to the beauty of something
simple or different than us.

Art can be therapy just like anything else.

Intention:
How do I use art in my life? How do I see art?

# 216. Pick A Country

Not every day.
but like today maybe.

Look at a map and pick a country
where you aren't even sure what language they speak.
Even someone with a degree in world politics
or geography can do this.

*Because we don't know everything.*

Spend a minute learning outside of the news,
outside of politics, outside of anything.
Spend a second finding out about the religion,
history and culture of this place.
Do this for the sheer Disney-It's-a-Small-World
1960s innocence of it.
Find out how the journey of these people will move you.
File away that love for a rainy day.

Intention:
Will I take a minute to learn about something
for the sake of learning?

## 217. Remember The Path

Excuse me– I'm a little busy
with my geography homework.

The point of this culture and 1960s idealism phase
is to develop a greater sense of the world around us.
To gather a little bit of awe about this planet.
To give us more than just our day-to-day drudgery
as a reason to move forward.
To get us excited about the Path.
The Path is there for us to become.

*Become what?*

Become whatever you are meant to be.
When you are easing on down the road,
it is important to open yourself to all your options.

Living in fear of the world is not an option.
For those of us who have traveled and are worldly,
it is to remind us of what we don't know
and remind us what is important
about seeing the amazing, big world.
That is to say, remind us to stay humble and open
on the Journey so that jaded senses don't miss anything.

Intention:
Are we open to all of the things on our Path?
Do we see world with awe?

## 218. Fall Into Something You Love

*Not someone, right? Something.*
*Doesn't seem like as much fun.*

All sorts of things can give your life meaning and purpose.
Allowing yourself to find the things that you love to do,
or be a part of, are just as important as your family
or other deeper meaning themes.

How does that girl know how to grow up to develop
her own sense of self and contentment
if she never saw her mother do it before her?
How are you supposed to become the person
you want to be if you don't ever allow yourself
to fall in love with life?
What is the Journey for if not to fall into love with life?
And how do we fall in love with life,
without loving some things along the way?

Intention:
Do I allow myself to enjoy myself?
Do I allow myself enough to investigate what I like to do?

## 219. Investigate Something Someone Else Loves

Why?

We can learn a lot by looking at people who we admire and the things they do. There is no shame in that.

*You get to be who you want to be.*

If you see someone who is really different from you,
but they are just plain cool in every way you admire,
you can look at what they do.
Now, this isn't to say be a copy cat,
obsessively dressing and imitating them.
Just look around and don't be afraid
to try something new based on what you have seen others do.

It doesn't matter how cool someone is, or how together they seem, they have gone through more than one iteration of their personality and habits. You are on a Path that allows you to change and grow whenever you want.

Look around, investigate, and do.

Intention:
Am I afraid to try something different?

# 220. Smile At Everyone

## And Mean It.

The "mean it" part is pretty crucial.

Sincerely acknowledging people around you
does a lot for your soul.
It also makes others feel loved and appreciated
way more than you even intend.
This simple action gives back so much more than it takes to do.
Day to day can suck our well dry of kindness.
The weird thing is the way to fill that well is to just give it out.
People are insecure, scared, and full of crap
just as much as the rest of us.
Sincere kindness is the gift that will rebound on you
in ways you can't even imagine.
Develop a sense of sincerity with the people in your world
and see how you benefit over time.

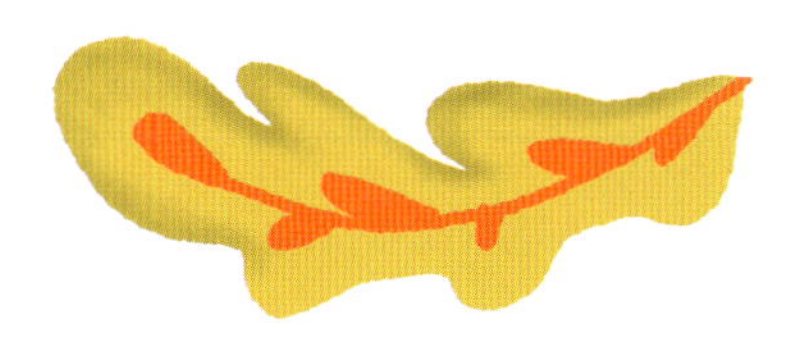

Intention:
Can I sincerely reach out to people?

## 221. Just Love People

*Smiling was pushing it.*
*this is a bit much to ask.*

Every great spiritual leader preaches
the theme of do unto others.

Start there.

The meme game around
'everyone is on a Journey' is phenomenal;
you are likely familiar with what is being said here.
Let's take it a step further, of course.
What if everyone adopted this mentality?
What if the revolution was about compassion?
What if true compassion for people
who are genuinely different than you
opened your heart in a way that busted down your own fear.
Everyone feels misunderstood, isolated,
or threatened at some point.
Like Russia and the U.S.
pointing nuclear war heads at each other,
we are working toward mutually assured destruction
when we act like this.
Don't be a part of the standard war games
of black and white thinking.
See your part in creating that distrust, bias and fear.

Join the rebellion: Compassion is revolutionary.

Intention:
Really, can you love people?

# Remember To Live

# 222. Take A Vacation Day

Praise Above –
that was getting heavy.

While we are busy becoming the best us,
saving the world,
and generally working on every damn aspect of our lives,
we can feel a little bogged down, to say the least.

Balance is also the best practice on the Path.

Otherwise, we are going to fall down
in too many aspects of our lives.
That bitch in our head is going to start yaking at us again.
The negativity takes over any kind of compassion
and the next thing you know you are drowning
in Moon Pies, Doritos and rosé.

It's okay. Have compassion for yourself.
Practice non-violent thinking.
You need a break. Take one.

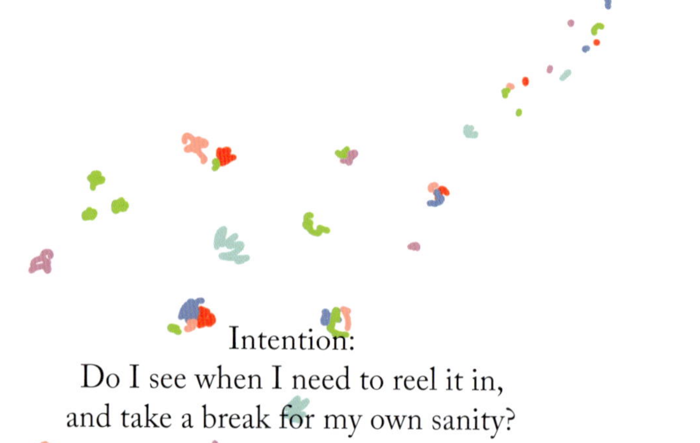

Intention:
Do I see when I need to reel it in,
and take a break for my own sanity?

# 223. Plan A Little

GIRL - my Planner Game is on Point!

Yes, but maybe plan a little for your dreams.
Plan a little for your sanity.
Plan a little for your mental health.
Life is what happens while we are busy with our days.
If we want something to happen differently,
we have to Plan a little to see that come to fruition.

Take the time to Plan for something other than tasks.

Let yourself be a part of a bigger Plan that is just for you.
Then, you can actually see it happen.

Intention:
Do I dream without Plans?

## 224. Be Spontaneous

That is how I ended
up with my 3RD Child...

Okay, maybe not just in the sexual arena.
Although, that is great
(we love that you have a happy sex life),
but we are talking about day to day.
In order for the world around us to change,
we must change the world around us.
Take the road trip, buy the tickets, call your girls
(or boys!) (or gender non-conforming folk!),
buy the puppy, sell the house, do the thing.
Sometimes the only thing standing in your way
is obstinance and lack of forward momentum.
Give yourself a little push, every once in a while,
and do the thing you are thinking about.

*Stop laboring over it.*

The magic happens when you take the leap of faith.

Intention:
What is stopping me? Can I just do the thing?

## 225. Look At What Makes You Happy

GIRL - I don't even Know.

Look at what makes you happy so it can fortify you when you are not happy. This is for when you want to wrap misery around you like a warm blanket. We spiral and lose our way. We need a hard stop of self-love and self-care*. We need tools to drag us back up. We need to be okay with that. Find out what the things are that make you happy. Care enough about yourself to do that so that when the negativity begins to take over, you have a lifeline. Fill your toolbox with a thousand little things, so you can face a spiral when it hits. Then do just one of them.

Don't play guilt.

Guilty pleasure is there for precisely this reason.
Then do another.
Then start to feel the feels and the positivity.
Then smile and maybe get back up.

*(*All severe mental health issues should be managed by a professional. That is encouraged and validated here.)*

Intention:
What is in my toolbox that makes me happy?

## 226. Look At Who Makes You Happy

Harry Styles -
Harry Styles makes me happy.

Great! But…
Maybe a little closer to home.
Look around you.
Do we hang around people who bring us up in life?
Do we stay in relationships because of obligation?
Do we know how to create boundaries with toxic people?
Why is it so hard to cut toxic people out?
Are the relationships in our lives the ones we want,
or are they dragging us down?
Ultimately, we teach people how treat us.
If we put up with crap in our lives, then
we show others and ourselves to treat us this way.
If we allow people to rob our minds of our sanity,
we are valuing that toxicity over our own happiness.

Look at who makes us happy in our lives
and look for more of those people to include
in our little band of merry maids.
Look for those who support and uplift you.
Look for those who want your success and happiness.

Ultimately all of those decisions are ours.

Out with the toxic and in with our supportive sisters!

Intention:
Do I know how to surround myself with the right people?

## 227. Know That Happiness is Based on Choices

BUT you Don't understand...

But we do.
And we know life can be hard.
We know anxiety and depression are real.
We know substance use disorder.
We know death.
We know people who have had everything stripped away and gotten back up.

We also know the choices you make to get help are the choices that change your reality. We know that you can choose to either stay in one place or get up and get help. We know that you can stay in one place or you can make a plan. We know that the definition of insanity is doing the same thing over and over and expecting different results. We know you have choices and ultimately only you can make them. We know if you drown in what you see as your unique suffering it will bring you vast misery. We know you can choose differently. You can see yourself as part of the solution. You can drag yourself kicking and screaming to that meeting. You can drag yourself to that interview. You can make yourself do that little bit on your project. You can pick up the phone and call the counselor. You can walk away. You can walk toward. You can make better choices. You can love yourself enough to make good choices. You can become. You can create your Path. You can get better.

Intention:
Do I see my pain as unique?
Does that prevent me from making good choices?

# 228. Play, Play

Right- cuz after Reality check #227
I need some air.

Let's be real,
even in the middle of the hardest times of your life,
you need a break for endorphins.
In fact, you need them more in those moments.
Stock up on laughter and exercise,
and play to bolster your reserves for the harder times.
What do you do to play?
Sports, gaming, cards, art museums, shopping, Zumba, yoga,
spirit circles, church groups, hiking, zip lining,
skiing, sledding, dancing?
Who cares? Do something fun!

Balance is play on the Path for strength in hard times.
Get your game on!

Intention:
Do I know how to play? Do I have games in my life?

## 229. Rest, Rest

This I can do.

We are talking more about balance here.
If you are going to expand your emotional and spiritual mind,
you need rest.

If you are doing the things and making the plans
and trying to move and,
oh yeah, taking care of your kids, or dogs, or cats,
or partner, or everyone at work, or whomever,
you may be a little tired, thank you very much.

And sometimes you are about done
with this mental health thing
and this Path thing and all the talky talk.

And you just can't think straight, and you start to spin.

Lay down. Breathe.

Feel the breath going in and out and simply focus on that.

Rest. Let it go and keep moving through.

There is no perfection here.
There is no perfect prescription.
There is all of us walking along our Journey
doing the best we can.

Today, the best — is rest. And that is perfect. Do that.

Intention:
Do I know how to rest when I need it?

## 230. Make A Coffee Date

*I prefer fairly traded chai with hand crushed stevia leaves...*

Good, good. That works, too.

The point is that she wants to hear from you as much as you do.
Just call and make the date.
Connect. Re-connect.
We make our circle what it is, and we won't be able to do that if we don't take the few seconds necessary to develop it.
A lot of us are busy. A lot of us are spread thin.
All the more reason to reach out. Just call and check in.
Call and make the date.
Do the things that help create your band of merry maids.
Too many times connections with good people are lost because we just don't have the time, or we are afraid.

Neither reason is a good one.
Make the call.
Give that relationship the chance you want to give it.
Then, enjoy your chai!

Intention:
Am I afraid to reach out?
Do I devote time to connecting with the people I want in my life?

## 231. Go To 'That Place' For The Day

What place?

Is this a metaphorical curse?

Mindless wander through whatever.
The mall, the cider mill, the art museum,
the city center, the park.

Go where there are people,
and be a part of the world.
We have been isolated so many times,
whether by circumstance or by choice.
We can only see the beauty in other people
when we actually see them enjoying themselves.
Be a part of that joy.
See the world.
Celebrate the crowd rather than fight it.
See the colors and smells.
See the people.
See how this simple trip reminds you how wonderful
it is to be out with others in this amazing world we live in.

Intention:
Can I use simple moments to celebrate the world I live in?

## 232. Believe In Self-Care

Yeah-Yeah-Yeah...

We know you know because this is #232 of the Path.
But don't just give it lip service. Live it.
Remember self-care really isn't just the occasional face mask.
It can be that, but it is more of taking the time to care for yourself in a way that benefits you.
Self-development, self-knowledge, self-drive.

It is caring enough about yourself to want more for you.

It is loving yourself enough to allow for your own success.
It is understanding that you deserve happiness and fulfillment.
It's caring enough about yourself to put the time in and develop the grit. It is caring for your Path, because you are the only one who can.

Intention:
Do I care enough about myself to allow myself to become the person I want to be?

# 233. Sing Really Loud

What the Hell?

Or scream, or shout, or recite Shakespeare.
But, actually, sing.
This is to release every inhibition
you can possibly have
and, really, to bring you some freaking joy.

Sing with a crowd.

Tell everyone to sing in their best out-of-tune voice.
Sing because there is something elemental and pure about it.
Sing because haters gonna hate and you don't care.
Sing for yourself and for the pure joy of it.
Sing the song that makes you cry.
Sing the song that makes you dance.
Sing in your kitchen.

Just sing.

And when someone else sings, join in for fun.

Intention:
Can I allow myself to be open enough to sing out?

## 234. Remember To Live

*"I'm not living to die. Gonna stand in the wasteland,*
*look you in the eye."*
*~ Brandi Carlile & Alicia Keys*

Choosing to live prevents the alternative: living to die.
When we feel empty, like a shell,
we forget to live in the moment.
We forget joy and beauty and people and singing.
Conscientious happiness happens because we work toward it.
We remind ourselves of the beauty around us.
We reach out to people and connect.
We see the goodness in the world.
We remember to use our tools to move through pain
and avoid spiraling.
We remember to live with the goal
of staying on the Path.
This remembering to live
is choosing to do more than just exist.
These choices are what make the difference.
They drive us toward a better place,
toward a better existence,
toward contentment.

It is that drive that ultimately makes you happy.

Intention:
Have I made the choice to live?
How do I choose to live?

# Remember Girl-Power

# 235. Look For Your Truth

Save me the time -
& just tell me.

We can't cheat on this.
We need to know who we are and what we believe.

Traditionally, men are taught this from an early age.
To know what their fiber is, their mettle, their worth.

Women flounder through taking care of everyone else,
barely giving themselves time for bathroom breaks,
let alone taking the time to develop a true sense of self.

We are on the self-care Journey.
If we are going to define our own Path
it is pretty darn important to know who you are,
what you believe, and why.

This will only help define our goals and dreams.

This is vital to your success,
because you aren't going to commit
to something that isn't part of your truth.

So get on it, sisters and others! Find your truth!

Intention:
Do I know myself? Do I know my truth?

# 236. Read Something Other Than This

Like #237 -
OR an entire other book?

We spend a lot of time investigating
who we are and what we enjoy.
This is important because on the Path, we evolve.
We don't just spend time looking at self-improvement.
We read about our professions.
We read drama and romance.
We read science-fiction and fantasy.
We read history and culture.
We read about women who inspire us.
We can also read for actual fun.
We read what we want to
and learn what we want in the process.
The world is this big, amazing, diverse, and beautiful place.
As we are moving along our Path,
take some time to enjoy learning about it,
and enjoy the fantasies that come out of it.

This is another form of self-care.

Not sure where to begin?
Make a list and pick what you can have fun reading today.
:)

Intention:
Do I take time for my mind? Do I enjoy that?

## 237. Understand Belief Grows

*"I have a voice, it started out as a whisper, turned into a scream"*
*~ Alicia Keys and Brandi Carlile*

Everything that is important to us
was just a glimmer at one point.

*We learn. We grow. We change.*

Think of the amazing things that will come to us over time. This is the secret of walking down your Path. You get to grow and change at any age. You get to become what you want to be at any time. Belief in a way, cause, or spiritual practice (or even ourselves) grows over time as we feed it.

We don't just wake up one day completely healed from our traumas and trials and fears. We have to work through that. We have to walk a while before we run. This is exciting news. You don't have to know it all. You can begin with a whisper.

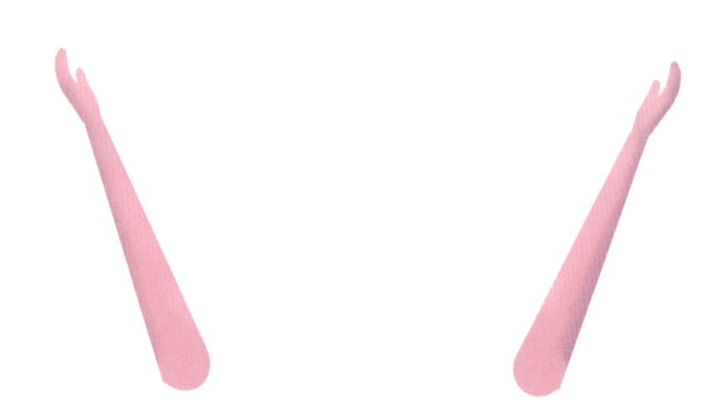

Intention:
Do I let fear of not knowing stop me from growing?

## 238. See How Your Beliefs Have Changed

*I was so much older then, I'm younger than that now.*
*~ Kris Kristofferson*

Look back at what you thought ten years ago.

Were you convinced of yourself then?
Did you know something that is patently untrue to you now?
Review the history of your beliefs.
Sometimes, we are wrong.
Sometimes we are taught a different perspective
and we change the way we see things.
This review of our past beliefs
allows us to approach the world
with a little more kindness and understanding.
If this is true for you,
think of how many things you think you know now,
that will inevitably change.
Now, this isn't to say second guess yourself.
No, no, no…that is just living in fear.

You have no idea what the future holds.

*Be assuredly you.*

Just know that everyone has these changes in their lives.
Extend the same grace to them
as you would want someone to give you.

While you are at it,
make sure to forgive yourself as well.

Intention:
Do I approach people who think differently than me with grace, or do I expect them to think exactly like me?

# 239. Look At The World Like A Child In A Sandbox

Do I get naptime & Snacks?

Think about how amazing it is that we put a child
in a pile of dirt,
and they sit there and create a world.

Seriously.

What if we looked at our own world that way?

Instead of drudgery, what possibilities face us each day? Perspective changes like this don't happen because we are born with sunshine coming out our posterior. They happen because we choose to see the world this way.

You know what happens then?

You get to be more amazed. You get to be more content. You get to learn and see instead of just existing. Next time you are facing a day and feeling like it is all a bore, look into the dirt and see what you can create.

Intention:
Can I create my own world?

## 240. Listen

*If you are a listener, then allow someone to listen to you!*

We tend to be either good listeners or good talkers.

There is truly nothing wrong with that, but stretch yourself. Listen to people intently all day. Practice listening so that you don't miss the good bits when they come by. If you are the listener, then share a little. Take the risk and talk. Get that inside-your-head stuff out in the open. Chances are, it needs a little airing.

Take time to do the opposite of your nature, so that you are good at both. People who talk, sometimes miss important moments. People who listen, sometimes let their inner thoughts go amuck. Switch it up. Learn to do both well.

That way the thoughts don't get toxic in your head, AND you won't miss the good stuff.

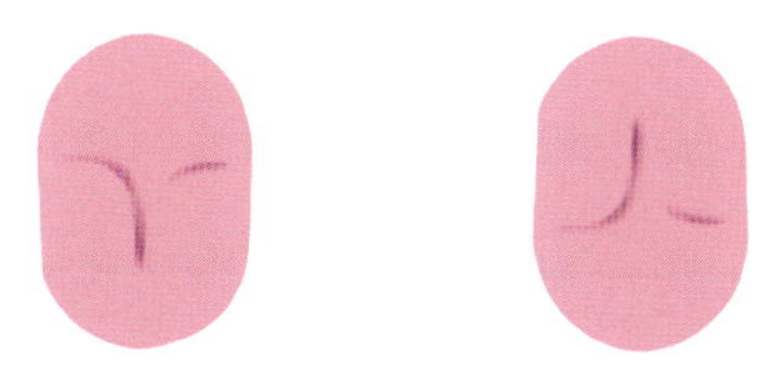

Intention:
Am I a listener or a talker? Can I switch that up?

## 241. Respect Yourself, Respect Others.

*"A good leader inspires people to have confidence in the leader, a great leader inspires people to have confidence in themselves. "*
*~ Eleanor Roosevelt*

First, we respect ourselves. Then we can respect others.

When we learn how to respect ourselves,
we don't need the approval of others.
We can pay it forward.

The order of this is important.

Work toward teaching yourself to be respectful of yourself. Do the things that make you proud of yourself. This doesn't mean being shocking or bitchy or dramatic.

This means taking the steps that create the You that you want to be, so that you don't have to do the other things just to feel alive. We usually don't even recognize how we disrespect ourselves. Some of us are constantly sorry. Some of us scream at others. Some of us use shock value. Some of us just don't even try. Let's start respecting ourselves enough to become the women we want to be. Then we can build those up around us and watch them fly too!

Intention:
Do I respect myself? Do I care enough to encourage myself?

## 242. Develop Beliefs

Don't just believe what you want to.

It is certainly easier to just believe what feels good and right to you, but that isn't helping anyone in the long run. When you feel something should be right, it is easy to believe that meme that backs it up 100%. Whatever your beliefs, check them.

*Unfortunately, the world just isn't that cut and dry.*

There isn't one great Sauron the Deceiver or Regina George out there that we can all hate, and one great Hobbit hero or Janice Ian we can stand behind. Hate is easy and, sometimes, even feels good, but it eats away at our soul and is not constructive. Find compassion for all people so that when you hear something laced with hate, you can investigate it openly without bias.

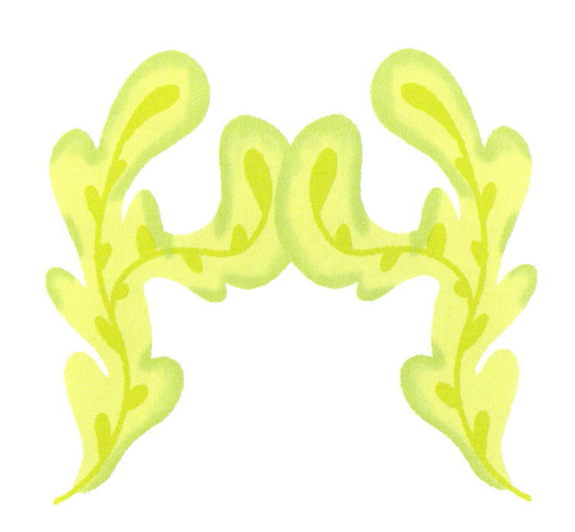

Intention:
Do I take time to consider what I believe?
Do I believe what I want to believe
without considering all sides?

## 243. Build Her Up

*Every Single One of Us.*

Calling all sisters and others: We need you to be kind to each other! Think of how incredibly strong women could be if we built each other up regularly. That kind of giving comes back to you tenfold. Instead of focusing on your own insecurities, think about encourging others around you to be better. Think how empowered all those women get to feel just because you got outside of your head and believed in them. Then, you get to feel pretty awesome because you are a part of this kiss-ass circle. All the angst and fear that comes out sideways as jealousy, hatred, and meanness is converted into power; Power for you, and power for those around you.

Intention:
Do I let my insecurities make me mean?

# 244. Do Self-Centered Self-Care

Manicures & Facials ?

Taking a day is nice,
but how about you take your life and do You.
Yes, we all have to pay our bills and do the things.
We can also make sure that process doesn't involve
a pathological level of self-abuse that isn't helping you,
isn't helping your loved ones,
and certainly isn't exampling how to live.
Self-care is understanding
that you cannot be any good to anyone else,
until you are on a Journey to your best you.
We give of ourselves too much
without ensuring that we have the foundation.

Build your foundation.
That is self-care.
That is what you really deserve.

Intention:
Am I building a foundation for myself?

## 245. Don't Excuse Yourself For Being Human

But - this is Not an Excuse
to Not be Polite -

It is not your fault someone else tripped.
It is not your fault someone else is not on a Journey.

It is not your fault.

Remember:
They might just be an asshole, or you might be a tad insecure.

Dig deep, here.

Look at why you feel it is necessary to apologize all the time.
Why must we berate ourselves in our heads
as well as outwardly?
Why is that bitch in your head still harping on you?
You are on this journey and you are killing it.
No one else can define your Path except you.
You do not need to apologize anymore.
You need to speak out and know your worth.

Intention:
Instead of apologizing for my existence,
can I celebrate my Path?

# 246. Pull Out Your Inner Witch

*"If you have yet to be called an incorrigible, defiant woman, don't worry, there is still time. "*
*~ Clarissa Pinkola Estes*

The inner witch is the bad ass self-assured girl.
This witch will call on her strength to speak her truth.

Nevertheless, they will try to silence her.

She will continue with determination to walk her Path anyway.
The inner witch is the one who has done the work
to become the sister, or other, that she wants to be.

We are at any number of phases on our Path,
and sometimes we are still working on the ability to call on her.
She is not the shock-value mean-girl who speaks her fear.
(This girl has great value
but is in a different place in her Journey).
The inner witch doesn't need drama
or fear-based responses,
because she knows her worth.
She can respond to negativity
without needing to explain herself.
She is the mother, the maiden, and the crone.
She has seen too much of this life
to submit herself to subjugation.

Sometimes, she can fly.

Intention:
Do I value myself enough?
Am I working toward inner strength?
Do I know other women who show this strength?

## 247. Remember: Girl Power

There is the SPARK of something
TRULY Beautiful
& POWERFUL
in every single one of us.

The US (women's) soccer team winning.
Wonder Woman.
A group of five-year-old girls
in a huddle after a t-ball game yelling "girl power".
A group of women out together just thrilled
to be letting loose for a night
without a need for anyone but themselves.

One hundred years ago, these superhero moments
weren't something people imagined.
Women had just gotten the right to vote.
Women have a lot of catching up to do.
Let's never again be that divided from each other.
Remember to celebrate the attributes of the feminine.
When women say, "I hate working with women",
they fail to recognize this is a form of self-hatred.
When women deny other women, they hurt themselves.

*"When women hate on other women, everybody loses."*
*~ Girl, Donna Missal*

The path is about empowerment, not divisiveness.
Anyone who has ever been left out of the game
can understand how important it is to be supportive of each other.
We embrace self-empowerment. We embrace supportive
community. We embrace girl power!

Intention:
Do I see how my attitude towards others can hurt me?

# Heal

## 248. Recognize The Trauma

What are the HARD STOPS
in your history?

When you look back at what brought you here today,
there are distinct moments that pop in your mind.

*They are there for a reason.*

They are there because they help define you.
If you look back honestly,
many of these are the moments you need to revisit and heal.

Have you done a thorough cleansing of that history?
Do you give the idea lip service,
but don't really dig through all the baggage
associated with these moments?
Do you see yourself as unique in this pain?
Be assured that you are not.

Maybe your situation and history are specific to you,
but certainly the response to emotional pain is universal.
Universally it should be shared.

Without going through some sort of soul cleansing,
we really can't move forward.

Intention:
Have I worked on my history?
If I have, do I continue to work toward keeping the slate clean?

## 249. Work With Someone Or Something

We really don't Know
How to do this Alone.

There is such a tremendous history
of the need to share with others.
We would be remiss in denying this history.

Also, like all directed goals,
this doesn't happen magically without guidance and structure.
It can be a very groovy, loose type of structure,
but something else outside of our own brilliant self-guidance
is necessary to hold us accountable.

Whatever our personal goals are,
in the beginning of that Journey,
we can draw on those people who have gone before us,
and derive our Path from theirs.
Whether that is through some sort of program
or some kind of personal guidance,
we need others to help us along.

Then, someday,
we get to help others along.

That is HOW IT WORKS.

Intention:
Do I have the guidance that I need? Where can I go to get it?

## 250. Read Books By Powerful Women

We Can Do It.

There are just too many to mention here:

Alice Walker, Toni Morrison, Barbara Kingsolver,
Isabel Allende, Margaret Atwood, Amy Tan, Maya Angelou.

We could go on all day about women authors that are badass today, but these are some of the Godmothers of this generation.

Find and support women in literature, music, and art.
They will identify pain on a level that is guttural, transparent, and vulnerable. This is how they have become powerful women. Look into that kind of wisdom to identify your own place in your Journey. These artists, wordsmiths, and musicians can be your modern day fairy godmothers if you let them in.

Intention:
Have I seen the amazing work powerful women have put out there? Can I see how this can guide my own Journey?

## 251. Stand Up For Yourself

So that you know
how to stand strong for others.

Who doesn't hate conflict? It is hard and messy.
Unfortunately, we cause so much of the conflict in our lives
by trying to avoid it.

The key is to be transparent about your position.

You could avoid so much conflict in your life
if you would be straight forward
about your position in the first place.

Standing up for yourself doesn't mean
you have to get in someone's face and be ridiculous.
That is completely unproductive,
and only hurts you in the long run.
It means clearly stating your opinion
when that moment happens.
It means not walking away thinking,
"I should have said something."

It means not trying to manipulate people to do what you want them to do, rather than simply telling them. It means owning your own stuff, and letting others own theirs. It is so much easier to stand up for yourself than to complicate your life with all the other choices.

Intention:
Am I transparent in my relationships?
Do I try to manipulate situations?
Can I simplify by standing up for myself?

## 252. Empty Your Soul Of The Fight

Whoa Whoa, hold on here —
I am a BAD ASS Bitch.

Badass bitches aren't badass because they are always up for a fight.
They are badass because they know who they are so well,
they don't need to fight.
They are assured.
They have gone through a cleansing process.
They have faced their own personal demons down,
and sliced that shit wide open.
That is what makes them badass.
They have given in to the concept
that it is better to be healthy and happy
than it is to stay stuck.

They have gone through the process of becoming that woman.

It is that Journey and that Path,
specifically, that makes them badass.

So, stop fighting yourself.
Stop standing in your own way.

Give up that fight and start the process of Becoming.

Intention:
Am I my own worst enemy?

## 253. Forgive Without Losing Yourself

*Forgive. So the pain doesn't eat you alive.*

Wikipedia says: Forgiveness is different from condoning, excusing, forgetting, pardoning, and reconciliation.

We can Forgive,
but we don't have to trust again.
We don't have to reconcile.

In fact, after we Forgive someone for something
that has been burning at our soul,
we often feel a profound indifference.

This is not Forgiving someone, and allowing them to return
to a place where they can hurt you again.
This isn't Forgiveness, it is insanity.
It is obsession. It is wishful thinking. It is folly.

If this is a relationship that can be reconciled, great!

We are no longer victims,
we move through pain.

So, the Forgiveness is for you to free yourself.

Intention:
Do I see how Forgiveness can free myself from my own pain?

## 254. Walk It Off

*Sometimes when we are drowning a little in trauma or pain,*
*it knocks us flat for a minute.*

That is OKAY.

But, at some point, we have to get up and walk it off.
Get back on the Path.
Drag ourselves out of bed,
and do the one thing that will help us see
a Path that doesn't involve pain.

Maybe that means finally calling for help.
Maybe that means doing one task toward a bigger goal.
Maybe that means organizing your earrings.
Whatever it is, sometimes just getting up
and doing one damn thing is what we need to do.

Then we get to feel just a little bit better.

Intention:
Do I know when to walk it off?

# 255. Talk To Them

*No one is inside your head*
*and therfore they cannot read your mind.*

When you are thinking, 'they should just know',
you are wrong. They don't know.
That is why you need to talk to them.
Everyone is different this way.
Your experience leads you to believe
that showing up for work fifteen minutes early
is the absolute minimum for on-time.
Another person doesn't think twice
about being ten minutes late to relieve you.
This may burn you on the inside…
thinking that they should just know.

They Don't.

They are blissfully unaware at your seething anger,
and are broadsided by it.
Because you never talked to them,
you are the problem here.
This is a simple example of 1,000 ways
not talking to someone can turn into drama
that far exceeds the 30 second conversation
that could have happened to stop the drama in the first place.

Talk to them.

Intention:
Do I expect people to live inside my head?

## 256. Focus On Solutions

*You do not have to live in your suffering.*

Feeling pain and going through negative periods of our life is normal and healthy — choosing to let those moments keep us drowning in quicksand is not.

When you are afraid and overwhelmed
think of the absolute worst-case scenario.

Then, picture what you would do in reaction to that.
How you would solve that problem?
Then, take a deep breath and confront the situation.
What is the worst that could happen?

Oh, right, you already know,
and you have that handled.

In most cases,
you won't need your worst-case scenario back up plan,
but it is there to buffer your fear.

Intention:
Do I know how to focus on solutions rather than live in suffering?

# 257. Quit The Bad Things

*You are too smart.*

We all know the things that interfere with our health.
Our health care system is not a preventative one,
so we don't focus on health.

We focus on pills.

So here it is:
Smoking causes lung disease that is a terrible, ugly death
that will catch up with you at some point.
Morbid obesity will lead to heart disease, diabetes,
and a veritable cornucopia of joint and pain problems.
Drugs are fine for a minute, or for festivals,
but as an adult they are simply mind-numbing,
wastes of time, and if you can't cut them out
that is what you will become.
And to top it all off…Alcohol is a drug —
a socially acceptable one —
but a drug none-the-less.
So are a thousand other substances and activities.

The simple truth is,
that if something is interfering with your ability
to walk down the Path to Kick-Assville,
you need to quit it or cut back.

If you can't do that, you need help.
No denial on the Path. Face your demons.

Intention:
Am I denying how much something interferes with my life?

# 258. Fail At Quitting, Try Again

*No one said, "Quit everything and be perfect tomorrow!"*

We do say
recognize,
Try,
keep Trying,
forgive,
get back up,
Try again,
love yourself as you are,
love yourself enough to
Try again.

This is what life is about.

What the Journey is about *is* the Journey.
Some days the elevator, some days the shaft.
When it's not your day, we have learned
to pull out our superhero multi-tool
that will save us from the 56-floor drop.
Maybe as we fall into the net we created,
we learn how to spring out!
Not only will you save yourself from the fall,
but you can celebrate all of the new skills
you have acquired on the Path.

Just keep Trying.

Start to see the beauty in the moments,
then the Trying isn't so hard.

Intention:
Can I start to see Trying as a beautiful thing, rather than a chore?

## 259. Turn It Over

*Turn over the things we cannot handle*
*to something outside of ourselves.*

Create a mental box
then create a real box.
Write down a trial and put the trial in there.
Turn it over to your God/Goddess/Spirit/Energy.
Get it the hell out of your head.
The things that are out of our control,
that are driving us crazy,
need to go.

Understand that all of the work you have done
on developing this sense of something outside
of your own mind was made for this moment.

You cannot control everything,
so give up the things that you can't control.

Let go of them.

Turn them over to something else and say good riddance.

Intention:
Can I let go of trying to control the uncontrollable?

## 260. Heal

Use the tools,
do the things,
get better.

Healing is what happens naturally
while you are walking down the Path.
You cannot force Healing.
The amazing thing that happens
while you are trying and doing
and falling and getting back up,
is that Healing happens.

All of a sudden you look back,
and you start to see some progress.
You start to see how loving yourself enough
to care for yourself leads to small, amazing changes.

Keep Going

You have opened the door to self-discovery
and the maze is endless.

It doesn't matter,
because when you are done with the process
the game is over.

Better to be continually walking and discovering!

Intention:
Do I see how self-care has begun to creep into my life?

# Be Uncomplicated

## 261. Take A Quiet Day

*"Look at me, I'm in tatters! I'm a shattered"*
*~ The Rolling Stones*

Some days,
all the noise and commotion,
in and outside of our heads,
is deafening.

It wipes us to pieces.

'Quiet tools' to the Rescue!

Meditate, walk in the park, bird watch, yoga…
(did we mention meditation?)

Do the things that quiet your mind
and remember that all that stupid ass shit
we fill our heads with is just that.
Look at the beauty. Watch the animals.
See the simplicity of relationships.

Take your life down a notch.
Forgive yourself for being human
and needing a minute.

Breathe

Intention:
Do I know when I need a quiet day?

## 262. Stop Before You React

*Like stop, drop, and roll for the soul.*

This is really a muscle that needs a ton of exercise.

We all have things that trigger us.
We react and overreact,
then get sad or indignant.
Reacting rather than *responding* to a situation
causes the bulk of drama in our lives.

We have no control over the actions and behaviors of others.
We have complete control over how we react to them.

If someone you are forced to have contact with is whacked,
they will always knock you on your ass with their behavior
until you expect them to be 'whack-a-doo'.

When you expect them to come at you with both guns blazing,
you can be pleasantly surprised every once in a while when they
don't. This is better than being knocked on your ass every time.

Intention:
Can I learn how to respond rather than react?

## 263. Take Care Of The Physical Needs

*Some days it's all we can do.*

Rest, eat well, breathe, repeat.

If that is the best we can do today,
that is better than a lot of other days.
When shit is hitting the (real or emotional) fan,
take care of the basics.

Maybe take one minute for a healthy meal,
or a twenty-minute nap,
or a quick walk around the block,
or one or two things that will fortify your mind and/or body.

When the tornado surrounds us,
it is good to have a couple of things to ground us to safety.

You don't have to fix
Everything right now.

Right now you can be kind to your mind and your body
so that you can grow stronger and face another day.

Intention:
Do I abuse my body during stress?
Can I learn how to change that habit?

## 264. Call A Friend

*"When you're weary. Feeling small.*
*When tears are in your eyes, I'll dry them all."*
*~ Paul Simon, Bridge Over Troubled Water*

Don't do this life alone.

Don't sit in your shit and try to be brave.
Call someone. Reach out.
Feel the feels and let someone tell you it is okay.
Let someone help you sort through it.
Let someone help you untangle
what has gotten so tangled in your mind.
Let someone be a friend.
Develop those meaningful relationships in your life
so that you can have this lifeline.
Create your own family of friends.

Intention:
Do I know how to reach out to others?
Can I allow myself to try to feel vulnerable in front of others?

## 265. Clear Your Mind With Intention

But your intentions are questions—
that doesn't exactly clear my mind.

Right, so the intentions are actually the answers to the questions.
No one creates your intensions for you.
You do that all on your own!
What can you do to quiet your mind?
What tools do you have?
What simple thing can you focus your mind on just for today?

Finding an answer to any one of these questions
for where you are in this moment today — that is the intention.
At the simplest form, an intention can be something like:
'offer grace to everyone today'.

Whatever the hell THAT means.

The meaning is all yours, so it doesn't matter what it is —
as long as it holds meaning to you.
It is your offering for the day.
It is your minds work for the day.
It is your prayer for the day.
It is your magic for the day.
Work with intentions of your own devising.
Add these to your toolbox.

Intention:
How can I use this technique to clear my mind?

## 266. Don't Tell The Secret

*It isn't your story to tell.*

Telling someone else's confidence is like... stealing their magic.
They shared a piece of themselves,
and you sold it on the market
to the highest bidder for a cheap thrill.
It isn't your story to tell.
Don't tell it.

The other thing it does, is it lessens you.
When someone is telling you a secret about someone
that hurts you specifically,
don't waste a second on the subject matter.

Instead, look at the person telling the secret,
and wonder about their motivation.
What kind of desperation leads a person
to hurt you like that out of a need to make themselves feel better?

They are the real problem.
The subject matter is truly unimportant.

The secret teller knows what they are saying,
and they are the ones who deserve our scorn.

Intention:
Beware of people bearing others secrets. What is their motivation?

## 267. Fly Under The Drama Radar

*Stepping into the pit of drama is a soul sucking shit fest.*

This can be the hardest thing to do.
In fact, walking away from drama can ruin relationships.

But, thank the Lord! Do you really need those kinds of people in your life? The people that seem to have drama
following them at every turn?

Of course, we can be dragged in at times, but look at what choices you make to stay in the middle of the drama. These are the drama-oriented places you need to identify and cut loose.
These are also the drama-oriented *people* you need to identify and cut loose. Sometimes we are the instigators of drama.
We turn anxiety outward and blame others for our angst.

Stop that now.

You have a toolbox to handle that.
Walk with those that soothe your soul.

Be a drama free zone.

Intention:
Am I surrounded by drama? What is my part in that world?

# 268. It Really Isn't A Big Deal

Easy for you to say

It is.

Psychology Today reports research that says upwards of 91% of the things we worry about are irrelevant. Freaking 91 percent!

I think we can all spend a little time
looking in the mirror and saying,
"Okay, calm the f@#! down."

Yes, we can really say with more than 90 percent assuredness that it really isn't a big deal. You are your own worst enemy here.

They aren't judging you. This isn't going to happen. They didn't mean it that way. You aren't going to lose it.

They love you.

We need to learn to look at the world
with a whole bunch more Hope.
We just do the next thing in front of us,
then the next, then the next.
Let someone else develop the ulcer.

You are on the Path.

Intention:
Do I worry too much? What can I do to reframe how I see life?

# 269. You Are Not Misunderstood

*"Oh Lord, please don't let me be misunderstood. "*
*~ The Animals*

I mean, sometimes we can be situationally misunderstood,
but this "being misunderstood" thinking
leads us down the path to "Victimitus".

You may recall that "victimitus" is the condition of staying in suffering rather than going through it. We work through pain and trauma; we choose to suffer. If you have been through something awful you may feel pain for a long time.

Here is the kicker, you can choose to let that define you, or you can choose to let the *healing* be what defines you. Look at what else can define you, other than your perception of being hurt.

Look at how moving forward can define you. Look at how the next chapter of your life can define you. Look at how amazing you are without all that separateness. Jump in with both feet.

You aren't misunderstood, you are just choosing to stand apart.

Intention:
Do I believe my pain is more important than my happiness?

# 270. Believe In The Mystery Of It All

Is this one of those hippy dippy ones?

Come on! Remember?
It is the triad of mind-body-spirit that is the key to happiness.
That 'spirit' piece is really important.
It doesn't mean that you have to believe in anything
outside of the idea that there are things you don't know.

Feel awe over that.
Make this piece as simple as you need, but embrace it fiercely.
On some subatomic level there is mystery
that we haven't uncovered and that is amazing and awesome.

Let's go one step further:
let's call everything outside of our understanding
the "Realm of Mystery".
Because by definition it is.

Knowledge of our world is limitless,
there is no way to ever know it all.
Consequently, there exists an infinite knowledge
that we are unable to comprehend.
Is there something that can comprehend it?
It's knowledge, right? By definition it is knowable.

See, there is mystery.
Love the fact that it exists.
We can spend our entire lifetime trying to prove or disprove
infinite knowledge or concepts of God.
Or we can just be really excited at the possibilities of the world.
Maybe we are just energy and we level up in the game after we die.

Intention:
Can I celebrate the mysteries of life?
Can I have a sense of awe over the things I don't know?

## 271. Write A Poem, Write A Story, Journal Your Life

### Stretch that creative Pen.

Writing can be very organic.
It is a great way to see where your head is at.
Write a list at the very least.
Write to see where your thoughts go.
Write to be able to read it back.
See the state of your thoughts in front of you,
rather than letting them dance around upstairs in your mind.

Lay them out so you can clear the way for more thoughts.
Perhaps better thoughts.
Stretch your creativity.
Maybe lay the text out so that it drips off the page,
mirroring the way you are feeling.

Try a rhyme or a haiku!
Just write them down;
look at them now, or look at them later.

Allow yourself to stretch creatively as well as emotionally.

It just feels good.

Intention:
Do I write down my thoughts?
Can I try to stretch my creative brain?

# 272. Plant A Garden

*Metaphorically?*

No, in the literal sense.
Maybe not a whole garden.
Maybe just a flower. Succulents are nice.

Watch something grow; care for it.

Something simple that just requires a little water and sun,
that teaches you the utter basics
of consistent caring and consequence.

Take note of how the sprouts, leaves,
or flowering make you feel.

See how you invest in the progress of your little plant.
This is the metaphor.
This act of consistent caring
brings us such simple, pure joy if we let it.

Now, do the same for yourself.

As you care for your #plantbabies,
so too will you care for yourself.

Intention:
Can I simply care for something,
and take joy in its progress?

## 273. Be Uncomplicated

*"Chill out, what ya yelling for? Lay back it's all been done before."*
*~Avril Lavigne*

What sound advice from young, 2002 Avril.
It really has all been said and done before
in one way or another.

So, don't worry about how you are doing it.
The key is to be transparently and purely you.
What that means is:
learn to fall in love with yourself first, then be you.
If you are mired down with insecurities,
self-doubt, and self-loathing,
you tend to swim in all sorts of complicated relationships.

Love yourself enough to allow yourself to simply be you.
That way all the complications that stem from insecurity...

...just fall away.

Intentions:
Do I see how self-love allows for life to be so much simpler?

# Understand Interdependence

## 274. Know You Are Well And Truly Blessed

*"You wanna fly, you got to give up the shit that weighs you down."*
*Toni Morrison, Song of Solomon*

It is beyond difficult to see the good things in life
when you are struggling.
It is also difficult to struggle through emotions
when you are able to see all the good things.
The key is to practice gratitude daily.
Practice understanding the good things in your life,
and really valuing them.

Not just, 'I like this thing because it is cool and pretty'.
Look at what brings you peace and true joy.

Those things will be in your toolbox when life is hard.
These are the things you will go back to over your lifetime.
These are the things you can always be grateful for.

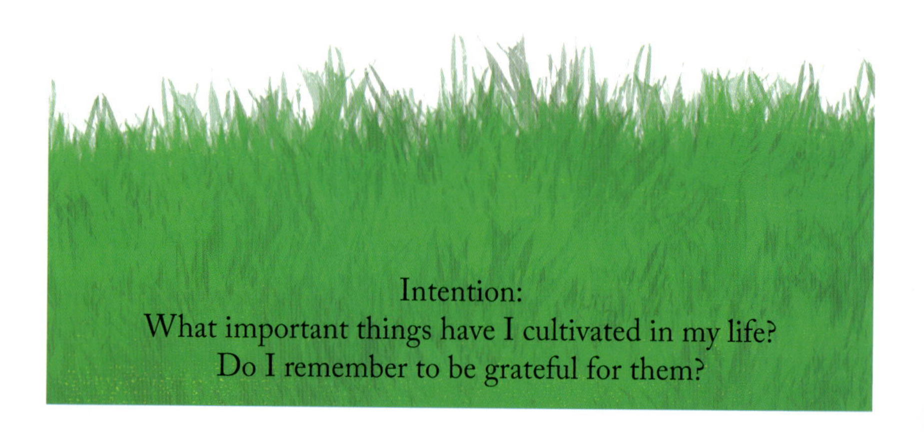

# 275. Give Up The Gut Reactions

But People ALWAYS say:
trust your Gut–

Sure, sometimes gut reactions are great,
and tell you not to walk down that dark alleyway…
or to not talk to that rude person you just met while out dancing…

You can learn to trust yourself, and keep your gut in check.

Because more often than not, in your day-to-day life,
the 'trusting your gut thing' is largely based on fear.
Let's go back to the fact that 91 percent of our worries are false.
Trusting your gut means that you are giving into fear.
This fear can frame how we see the world entirely.
Don't trust that! Look up the facts. Investigate.
Question people who have experience.
Believe experts in the field,
not your neighbor's brother, not your news feed,
not your entrenched religious, not political beliefs —
no matter what they are.

Squash the gut reaction theory and bring back the enlightenment.
Remember, they wanted to kill Galileo for discovering
heliocentrism—or in laymen's terms, that the Earth and other
planets in our solar system revolve around the sun.

Fear is not the ANSWER

No matter what your fears are,
question them. Confront them.
Do not feed them.

Intention:
Do I see how my fears have the ability to drives my beliefs?
Can I put my fear in the backseat and move forward
without that pit in my stomach?

## 276. Stare Into The Fire

Like a campfire, or a candle, or a fireplace?

You know how when you stare at a fire,
you can almost fall into a trance?
This is that magic or mystery.
It doesn't matter where you access that type of energy,
just know how to do it.
That place where you stare into the fire and,
almost without meaning to,
you clean out your mind.
This is a pure and simple form of meditation.

Try it. Even if it feels silly.

Just stare at fire, and see if you can access a quieter mind.
Add a little breathing. Or, better yet,
do something that puts you in contact with a fire —
like camping or lighting candles around a tub,
or, if you have access, light a fire.

Create spaces — that create peace.

Intention:
Do I know how create peaceful places in my life?

# 277. You Can't Fix Everyone

But- if everyone would just
listen to me!

If we spend our days worrying about everyone else,
we are missing the point.
We are spinning our wheels
trying to manipulate a force that is not ours to control.

We can be relieved that after only a few short years,
even parents can't control the actions of their children.
We can live by example. We can guide.
You can be the best possible you,
so that others can see how it's done.

But you cannot control them.

If you are spending a lot of time trying to control others,
you are likely avoiding what you should be doing for yourself.
There is no need to justify why you need or want to go down a
certain Path.

It's your path to go down.

Focus on that, and let everyone else worry about theirs.

Intention: Do I try to control others
at the expense of my own happiness?

## 278. No One Can Fix You

This is your Path alone.

A man, child, sister, or partner cannot fix you.
This is your Path, and you must walk it for yourself.
Other people can walk with you on the Path,
but they are there to be supportive.

Depending on people to take care of you will always fail you.
People are human,
and cannot perfectly care for someone else's needs.
We humans can barely take care of ourselves, sometimes!
We can share responsibilities for sure.
That is something different.

Understand this idea of sharing our lives
without becoming dependent in a way
that takes us away from our independent selves.
Without our own two feet, we cannot walk our Path.
If we are thinking that people in our lives owe us care,
if we think that people in our lives should be responsible for us,
we have lost ourselves.

People in our world can share our lives, help our lives,
but they cannot fix our problems.
By definition they are *our* problems.
So, start the plan, make the list, and walk your Path.

Intention:
Do I depend overly on other people
to take care of my problems?

## 279. Self-Care Fixes The World

Is this the modern day version of Live Aid?

This is the modern-day version of *Everything-Aid*.
This is a kindness that affects everyone around us.

If everyone could create a foundation within themself of strong self-care, the world would be in perfect harmony. We can't make everyone healthy though, so let's just make our little corner rock out with strength. Self-care is doing those things for yourself that feed the mind-body-soul triad. This creates within you an inner strength by building you physically as well as mentally. You get to face hardships head on, and not let them buckle your knees. You get to face that project, and not let it wipe your ass out halfway through the day. You get to be the person who can "handle it".

This fortifying allows you to be there for others. It allows you to do what you need to do, so that you get to do what you want to do. Somehow, we have lost track of how important this is for everyone. We mistake this as selfish. We see other "things" as more important.

This is the only thing that is important.
The rest, then, becomes easy.

Intention:
Do I see how nourishing my mind-body-soul
is the fundamental task in my life?

## 280. Faith Helps

Like - how much?

You have within you the key to your happiness. If everyone could fortify their daily life with a little spiritual something, this self-care thing would be so much easier. In a letter to a sixth grader's question about scientists praying, Albert Einstein said:

> *"Everyone who is seriously involved in the pursuit of science becomes convinced that a spirit is manifest in the laws of the Universe, a spirit vastly superior to that of man."*

This is the unknowable. This is what you can tap into if this faith stuff is hard for you. If you are reconstructing the faith of your youth, strip it clean to this level, then build it back up. Build it back up with awe and love. Know one thousand percent that *anything* fear driven is not helpful. Faith is the opposite of fear. Faith fills the hole that fear creates. Faith in the purity of the universe. Faith is a warm and loving God/Spirit.

You get to choose where you put your Faith.
When everything else in our lives fail, we can unabashedly
tap into the warmth, kindness, and love
that is the byproduct of Faith.

Intention:
Am I developing a Faithful practice that is the opposite of fear?

# 281. Community Is Important

*"None of us is an island, autonomous and independent from others. We can only build the future by standing together, including everyone."*
*~Pope Francis*

(on Twitter… seriously the Pope has a twitter account)

The modern world is amazing.
We get to choose who our people are.
We get to create a network of people we actually want in our lives.
We get to block people who are toxic.
We don't live in a pre-industrial world
that forces us to stay with people who are blatantly abusive.
We have that modicum of freedom in creating our community.
Make sure that the people in your life
are the people you *want* in your life.
We aren't saying you should dump everyone
at the first sign of trouble —
that is just cruel.
We are saying the opposite.

This Journey of self-care
strengthens your ability to "be there" for others.
They, in turn, get to strengthen and become better,
and be there for you when you struggle.

That is the Absolute Essence of Community.

Intention:
Is my community a safe place for me emotionally?

## 282. Everyone Struggles

Everyone is coming from Somewhere.

But not all the time, right?
This isn't to say that happy people aren't actually happy.

It isn't to say that everyone
is lying and walking around miserable.

Some people are,
but a lot of people are genuinely happy.

However, a lot of those people who are happy
have overcome shit you can't imagine.
(or maybe you can…)

It is what makes them happy.

If you have been strung out on heroin
and now you own a bakery,
you have some serious perspective
about what constitutes a problem.
We can learn so much from these people.
The grit we develop from overcoming adversity
is what makes us shine.

Tap into someone who shines, and learn from them.

Intention:
Do I see my struggles as obstacles to my Path?

## 283. You Are Not The Judge

*Who likes a Judgy McJudgy?*

*...Nobody.*

But also, judging other people eats away at our soul. We all have an Achilles heel in this area. No one is without their opinions. The key is to recognize that.

It is nice to be nice.

Also, too much of this kind of toxicity makes you ugly on the inside. It's a weak person's way of making themselves feel better. Work to identify those areas where you have a particularly hard time dealing with other people. Maybe write them down. Look at them. What do they say about you?

Is this the person you want to be?

Intention:
Do I let my opinions of others rule me?

## 284. Presume They Love You

*They are Not talking about You.*

REALLY. They are not talking about you
(Like 98% of the time).

The idea that this person is judging you,
or that person is saying something about you...
is actually very flattering.
The sadder truth of the matter
is that they probably aren't thinking about us at all.

We create these frenzies of fear
in our heads over other people's opinions.

The easier way to handle these toxic thoughts
is to presume everyone loves you
until they flat out tell you they don't.

But no need to worry.
They do love you.

Intention:
Do I live in fear of what other people are thinking about me?

# Be Present

## 285. Look For Common Ground

We can be in this thing together—

In 1985, the Cold War between the Soviet Union and the United States was quickly losing steam. The world was becoming just a little bit smaller, and people were tired of hating the Russians.

Sting famously sang the question
*'Do the Russians love their children too?'*, showing the ridiculousness of this kind of hate. This simple question can be applied to everyone in every situation. People aren't fundamentally monsters. There are individuals, of course, where circumstances have led them to do monstrous things, but those are the outliers. Thinking differently than us does not make people monsters, it makes them different than us. Stop looking for the differences. Instead, hone in on what you have in common with them. The world needs a lot more of this kind of understanding. Hate is just a byproduct of fearing what you don't understand.

Be magnanimous.
Be noble.

*Be the change you want to see.*

Intention:
Do I take time to try to understand people who think differently than me?

## 286. Understand Interdependence

Sounds metaphysical.

If we look at nature and see how everything has a balance and an interdependence, we can't help but see ourselves in this equation. If everything is connected, then everything depends on the health and well-being of everything else.

When we aren't working toward being a healthier person,
we don't just affect ourselves, but we affect the whole system.

Our family and friends are affected negatively;
our work is affected;
our ability to help others is affected.

Remember, this doesn't say we need to be perfect all the time.
It says we need to be willing.

We need to understand the importance of interdependence.
We need to be working toward a healthier self.
Just that little bit has a ripple effect within our community
that could move outward for generations.

Our tiny work towards a better self can be a stimulus for thousands of others. Don't sell yourself short! You are a part of something so much bigger than yourself. Understand that you make a difference.

Intention:
Do I see how my self-care is part of a greater world?

## 287. Give Up Your Fear Of The Future

*"Be afraid, be very afraid*
*But do it anyway. Do it anyway"*
*~ Jason Isbell*

How bad can it get?
Pretty damn bad.
Honestly, you can lose everything tomorrow.

The great news, is that everything can be rebuilt.
Look at the millions of stories of people
who have fallen below gutter level,
and rebuilt a kingdom for themselves.
This paralyzing fear of the future is the shackle that binds us.
The future will happen the way it will happen.
You cannot let this trap you in a constant state of fear.
What if you need to fall apart?
It is never the end of the world.

Usually, in fact, that is the beginning!

You just need to wander down the Path a little further
to see where the sunlight comes back.

Stop worrying about what will happen and start living for today.

Intention:
Do I let fear of what may happen,
stop me from moving forward in my life?

## 288. Don't Let The Flame Go Out

*"Make the most of yourself by fanning the tiny, inner sparks of possibility into flames of achievement."*
*~ Golda Meir*

We get tired some days.
The Path is about balance.
Within that balance,
it is important not to backslide until the flame goes out.
When we balance our days,
we can breathe and be present
while also remembering where we want to go.

This spark or flame is the reminder
that you are important.

That your Path is Important.

That you matter in the scheme of things.
Keep this inner flame within you always.
Let it be the compass that guides you forward.
Tend to it, even on those down days.

Especially on those down days-

This is the light that takes you through dark days.

Intention:
Do I tend to my inner flame?
Do I know what that spark is within me?

## 289. Close Your Eyes

*Seven appointments, eight-to-ten hours of work, four kids, dinner, assignments, due dates, yard work, bathroom cleaning, laundry, grocery, soccer, dance, grooming for the dog, shots for the cat...*

*...it is never easy to balance life.*

No One says it is.

But what is easy, with practice,
is quieting your mind, even for just a moment.

Close your eyes.
Picture yourself in a calm and beautiful moment.
Do not judge the thoughts that come to mind. Just acknowledge them and decide which thoughts are helpful to inner peace in this moment, and which are not helpful. Is thinking about all the work you have to do at home when you get home from work helpful for having inner peace? Probably not. Just try and lay that thought aside for now— it won't go anywhere. You probably will never have a fully quiet mind, but you can work to have a peaceful one.

Do an exercise like this regularly. Do this enough that it becomes habit. Quick realignment of your frenetic head helps with just about everything. In all of this chaotic reality, the sparkling quiet behind your eyes and your breathing is always with you. Don't forget to use them.

Intention:
Do I know how to quiet my mind and reboot quickly?

## 290. See Good Outcomes

*Don't be a Negative Nancy.*

You are with a group and planning something.
Then one person says,
*"but, what if"*.

Or you are looking at options
and the committee in your head says,
*"but, what if"*.

But *"what if"* what?
At some point you just have to dive in.
The committee can always come up with reasons to stay afraid.
At the current moment, *"what if"* can take a hike.

What if lightning strikes you tomorrow,
and you never did what you wanted to do?

Live a little more like that!
Live a little more in today,
and not in the potential 'badness' of tomorrow.

Intention:
Do I constantly second guess everything?

## 291. Plan For Those Good Outcomes

*"The future depends on what you do today."*
*~Mahatma Ghandi*

How do you prevent all of those "*what ifs*" from happening?
You plan the best you can.

You do what is necessary to move forward,
and then let the chips fall where they may.
We don't dive into everything with reckless abandon.

Luck favors the prepared.

The balance between preparing,
and moving forward is the ticket.
We can't stay in one place due to fear
of the infinite outcomes.
We also can't dive into a shallow pool
without breaking our necks.

Plan. Find a deeper pool. Have faith. And dive in.

Intention:
Do I move through things recklessly?
Do I let planning paralyze me?
Can I let go of both of these habits?

## 292. Play With The Dog, Cat, Or The Child's Hair

I don't have any of those things.

The point is — to do the simple things.
Allow yourself simple moments.

When we are spiraling up or down,
we can stop. Hard stop.

Look out the window,
and watch that bird for five minutes.
Look at how the world revolves and revolves
without your fretting.

Look how details in this very moment
are really quite incredible.
Use this as an exercise in your toolbox.

Nothing is ever as chaotic or impossible
as we make it out to be.
Sometimes the simple action of holding a kitten,
or smelling our kid's hair
will slow our breathing
just enough to ease us forward.

Intention:
Do I know how to stop and value simple things?

## 293. Don't Blink

This is a classic old lady lament
& it is literally impossible.

It has been said a thousand times before,
but time gets faster and faster and faster as you age.

Try to filter out what is important in life at any given moment.

This is a 'don't sweat the small stuff' thing.

This is the global understanding that,
in the scheme of things,
we have so little time on Earth.

This is a 'don't forget to do the important things well,
and don't worry about the other shit' thing.

This says that within any given moment
you have certain, meaningful things laid out before you,
and it is up to you to seize those moments.

This is your Path through your Journey.
You get to define it. You get to see what is really important.

The rest is for the birds.

Intention:
Do I know how to filter out the useless things,
and focus on the important ones?

## 294. Dream

And then do.

Living out your dream or passion
is not always perfectly possible.
However, you can't figure the Path out
unless you do the actual things.
So, you have a Dream.

Great!

What are the steps you need to take to make that a reality?
Half of them really suck.
Half of them aren't your passion or your Dream,
but they are necessary to make this Dream happen.

Along the way,
maybe you find you aren't that passionate about that thing,
but this Journey leads you down
another Path that you are excited about.

Guess what?

That is your passion now, and that is amazing!
The key is to keep moving forward
with what you want to do, and who you want to be.
Multiple Paths are always open to you.
As long as you allow yourself to Dream,
and take steps towards achieving that Dream,
this will all become clear.

No one's path is ever a straight line.

Intention:
Do I understand that Doing is the
backbone of Dreaming?

## 295. Call Your Mother

*Not going to call that toxic woman, you can't make me.*

So…maybe your mother, or, maybe another woman.

Make sure that you appreciate and check in with the women who came before you. Someone along the way showed you how to care enough about yourself to pick up a book about self-care.

We make our families what they are.
Your family—whether it is by blood or by choice—
is what you make it.

It is important to take the time to check in, and show some gratitude for the women in your life that made you what you are today. As time goes on, those women can help us understand that even the mistakes we have made are perfectly okay, because they have likely made a few of them too. They are bringers of wisdom and perspective.

They aren't remotely perfect,
but they have tasted time,
and know it's fleeting nature.

Intention:
Do I appreciate the people in my life who have guided me?

## 296. Don't Waste Time On Nonsense

*How much of our lives is a swirl of utter nonsense?*

People spinning in a quagmire of insecurities
will drag you in to their chaos
hoping to grasp some clarity for themselves.
That is not your job. Not your Path.
Not even on the horizon of your Journey.
These are someone else's irrational thoughts,
and you can choose to let go of them completely.
If chaos and nonsense surround you,
look at the source and cut it out.

Sometimes, the source of chaos is us.
If this is the case,
we need to get back into counseling.
We need to pull ourselves out of our own brains,
and get some perspective.
This is part of the Journey always.

Sometimes it is easier to block out
someone else's nonsensical thoughts, language, or actions.
Sometimes it's harder.

Sometimes it is easier to recognize
this behavior in ourselves.
Sometimes it's harder.

That's okay. We are human.
We do not achieve nirvana, and stay there forever.

We wax and wane on the mental health scale.
The nonsense around us is a good barometer.

Intention:
Am I surrounded by toxicity? What is the source?

## 297. Relate

That is so deep, Man –
I can totally Relate.

*Exactly!*
But seriously...
that is the thing.
Connect with people on that level.
Be transparent,
unafraid to share how you feel,
and be open to hear other people's stories.

This is how we become better.
This is how we fortify our Path.
This is how we learn
that the bitch in our head
is super mean and irrational,
and we actually aren't so bad after all!

Transparency helps us Become and helps others Become.

Become What?

Become the person we were meant to be!
Self-realization begins with sharing and relating.
It isn't some bad, doped out 70s film where "feeling"
isn't actually feeling at all.

It is plain and simple truth. It's connection with others.
And, in turn, it's connection to self.
Take the risk! Let it all out, sister.
This is how we become free.

Intention:
Do I understand that my own transparency
helps other as well as myself?

## 298. Tune In

*"I took a deep breath and listened to the old brag of my heart.*
*I am, I am, I am."*
*~ Sylvia Plath, The Bell Jar*

Take a few minutes to realize how people react
to and around you.
See how you react to them.
Notice your tone of voice.
Despite your intent,
see how those around you react.
You may not realize how you sound.
You may be tired,
and everything you are saying
is coming out a little wonky.
You may be more intimidating than you realize.
You may be a quiet person.
People may not be ignoring you to be hurtful.
They may have simply not heard you.

Other people in your life are in their own particular space,
and are doing their thing.
Tune into their reactions,
and understand that they are not about you.

Only your behavior is about you.

Tune into your environment,
and try to see where people are coming from.
Look in that mirror for a while.

Intention:
Can I tune into the people around me?
Can I see how I am reflected there? Can I see their struggles too?

## 299. Be Present

like show up
– or is this emblamatic?

Probably emblematic, but both are important.
Nothing can happen if you don't show up…
So, do that.

While you are there… be there!
Sometimes, we all spend a little too much time on our phone;
sometimes, we all ignore the moments around us.

Do you really need to drown yourself in that wine tonight?
Do you really need to sit on your phone
ignoring everything else around you?
Do you really need to check out of the situations
that make up the days of your life?

Check on that.

See if you can be more present.
See if you can check in, instead of checking out.

Life is what happens when we are participating.

Years from now,
you don't want to look back and think,

*where was I?*

Intention:
Do I participate in life, or do I tune it out?

# Work For It

# 300. Pump It Up

*"Without leaps of imagination or dreaming, we lose the excitement of possibilities. Dreaming, after all is a form of planning."*
*~ Gloria Steinem*

We have been on this Journey for a bit now.
Our Path is becoming uniquely ours.
We are focused, present, forgiving of ourselves,
and we know how to get back up if we fall.

Let's not forget to enjoy ourselves.

Look at any small piece of your Journey, and get excited.

You are worth every minute of happiness
that your life offers you.
Did you get up and do a little work on a project?
Did you move a bit, eat well,
not yell at those assholes
because it would be a waste of your beautiful energy?
Did you stick up for the person no one was thinking of?
Did you do anything you can focus on as improvement?

Get excited about that!

Now, plan a little more success,
and get excited about those plans.

Celebrate now and pump up for the future!
Let's get excited in here, and ease on down that road!

Intention:
Do I allow myself to celebrate the Path I am on?

# 301. Realize Magic Is What You Make

Magic, Music & Mayhem!
Now you're talking—

Clear off that table again.
Look around you. What do you see? What do you want?
What can you do to make your world a bit more magic today?
Maybe just place some sparkly lights and candles out.
Maybe journal about your dreams.
Maybe walk in nature and connect with beauty.
Maybe you just close your eyes, and let that magic seep in.

Let go of defeat.
Let go of that sinking feeling.
Let that negativity sink right into the ground.
Replace it with looking at all the possibilities in life.

Stop saying 'but I can't' and start saying 'yes I will'.

Put on your favorite song, sing out,
and let the magic come.

Yes. You. Can.

Intention:
Do you let yourself see the possibility in your life?

## 302. Tap Into The Spirit

*"The library is inhabited by spirits*
*that come out of the pages at night."*
*~ Isabel Allende*

Breathe in the air.
Let yourself be open.
Light the candle.
Take the bath.
Go outside and sit in nature.
Read a book from one hundred years ago
that is still relevant today.
Do something to remind yourself
that you aren't the center of the universe.

Feeling that kind of humility
helps us see the rest of our life as a gift.
Who cares about things not going perfectly
the way you think they should?
You get to be a part of this Journey!
You get to change your mind!
You get to rethink your entire life paradigm if you want.

None of the details of your life are so insurmountable.

Tapping into the spirit reminds us
that we can handle anything as long as our Path is fortified.

Intention:
Do I know how to fortify my Path
with a greatness that shows me my personal humility?

# 303. Set A Goal

Just one goal?

(Well, we have been a little grand here of late.)

Let's get back to basics.

We don't need to be perfect;
we just need to be okay with ourselves enough
to be able to tap into our own strength.
Little goals can help us feel better about ourselves
when we feel the weight of the world on our shoulders.
Bust down that weight into small bits.
Pick up one of them and say, "Today, this is my goal."

This mentality is powerful.

Every day you can do something like that.
You can build up your self-perception just a bit higher.
You get to build up your grit in a way that no one else can.
One small step at a time, on your road to Fabulous.

Intention:
Do I know how to handle myself when I feel overwhelmed?
How can I break things down into manageable pieces?

## 304. Let Go Of That Vice

Ummm – What Vice?

That one.

The one that takes you out of the world, and puts you somewhere imaginary. The one that prevents you from self-realizing. Maybe it is a substance addiction, maybe it's a video game.

Time to air it out, and put it away. If you can't, then it is time to get help. But if it is something you can put away, start putting it away. This vice serves to pull a veil over you. It separates you from your true self. It blocks your way. It doesn't help.

This can be the wine, but it can also be the 24-hour news cycle. It can be gaming or edibles. It is the thing that used to calm you, but now just takes time away from you. And if we are honest... it makes us feel a little guilty.

If it isn't an addiction, this is a matter of choosing yourself over an escape. It will always be there, just do it a little less!

Intention:
Do I need to cut back on something in my life?

## 305. Let Other's Do It Their Way

But my way is better!!

*Said the three-year-old.*

When we bash our head against the wall,
it is time to seek guidance.
If we are struggling to do something,
the only way to learn how to do it better is to get help.
Sometimes this is hard on us
when we reeeallllyy want to know it all.

This is the Ego —
the devil in disguise.

The Ego fights against the things that build up our ability
to move forward on our Paths.
This beastly little aspect of our personality
either tells us we suffer too much
and everyone else doesn't understand,
or that we know better, and they can't tell us what to do.

Tell this evil incarnation of our own personal downfall,
to go back to the hell from which it was spawned.

Listen to others that have gone before.
See their successes.
Learn the tools they used, and use them!
You don't need to know everything —
you need to be willing to ask and learn.

Intention:
Do I realize when I need help?

## 306. Persevere

*"To persist in a state, enterprise, or undertaking in spite of counterinfluences, opposition, or discouragement."*
*~ Merriam Webster Dictionary*

One flippin, trudging step at a time. Somedays we are flying to the moon, and others we are lucky to have shoes. Understand this is the way of life and how to Persevere.

You are not lazy, or stupid, or incapable.

You just have to get through this one day. Then, you can move on to the next. When you get through a couple of these difficult days, there are always easier days ahead.

Some days don't feel that way, though. Some days you feel the weight crushing on you like a boulder. Those are the days you persevere. Those are the days you draw on your toolbox and get through. You can do this! You know how! Persevere.

Intention:
Do I know how to handle those down days?
Can I draw upon the tools I have been learning so far on my Path?

## 307. Be Unexpected

Surprise Even Yourself.

There is no rule book that says
the person you were at 22
is the person you must be for your entire life.

*You are allowed to change.*

You can grow and change every year
if you allow yourself to do that.

In fact, you can wear a flannel on Tuesday
and six inch heels on Friday
(and then Saturday—you can decide to wear both!)

You can be laid back on Monday
and all get-up-and-go on Friday.

Nothing and no one need hold you to one way of being.

Locking yourself into a box only limits you.
Stretch your wings,
and see what you can become
by doing something outside your norm.

Be Unexpected.

Intention:
Do I allow myself to explore who I am?

## 308. Participate

...I participate in Netflix
- does that count?

We frequently feel powerless.
We feel unable to affect changes in our lives;
we may not even know where to begin.
Some of us feel this way professionally.
Some of us feel this way in our daily lives.
Some of us feel this way politically.
There are a million places in the world
where it is easy to complain,
and feel you cannot change your stars.
Here's a tip: Participate.
Get on that board or committee;
volunteer for an organization.
Be a part of the solution.

You will find that very few people
actually do the work to make the differences
that affect our lives.

You very much can be a part of solutions.
You will also find that you feel much more empowered
if you Participate.
This makes things like work way more tolerable.

So, next time you want to roll you eyes at some committee,
think again. You can (and will) actually make a difference.

Intention:
What changes can I be a part of?
What revolutions can I take steps to be apart of?

## 309. Notice The Color Purple

*"I think it pisses God off if you walk by the color purple in a field*
*somewhere and don't notice it. People think pleasing God*
*is all God cares about. But any fool living in the world*
*can see it always trying to please us back."*
~ *Alice Walker*

In the midst of all the doing and being,
notice what is around you.
Alice Walker in her book *The Color Purple*
follows the stories of women and men
trying to get by the best they can against insurmountable odds.

When we are struggling and working
and being all of the things we can be,
we need to stop and notice the color purple.

This simple moment allows us to gain perspective
about what the world is, and what it is showing us.

These moments are where the magic happens.
It is here that ideas flow and energy is restored to us.

Here, we gain perspective.

Intention:
Do I take time to see the beauty around me?
Do I have perspective?

## 310. Face Your Fears

*Yes, this is a mantra from a science fiction book.*
*Get over it, it's freaking awesome.*

Litany against Fear:

*"I must not fear.*
*Fear is the mind-killer.*
*Fear is the little-death that brings total obliteration.*
*I will face my fear.*
*I will permit it to pass over me and through me.*
*And when it has gone past I will turn the inner eye to see its path.*
*Where the fear has gone there will be nothing.*
*Only I will remain."*

~ *Frank Herbert, Dune*

You don't have to face your biggest fear
and send yourself into a panic attack today.
Don't go running head-first into a huge conversation
with your abusive father just because you want to face fear.

Alternatively, you don't have to go sky-diving
to prove you are brave.
You have to be ready to face certain fears,
and that's okay.

But the key is not letting the fear of everything in the world
dictate your actions, choices, and thoughts.
The key is making decisions for yourself
and working with your fear,
rather than letting fear control you.

Intention:
What small thing can I do today that will help me confront a fear?

# 311. See The Progress

But I want it. Now

We get frustrated when Amazon
can't deliver our desperately needed trinket
to us within 48 hours.

This land of instant gratification
makes it difficult to see progress in our lives.

We aren't sprinting through life;
if we are lucky enough, it's a marathon.

We need to see how far we've come.
Sure, we still have far to go, too.
But so what?
Keep moving forward.

Take a minute, though,
to be happy with what you have done so far.

Even if you had entirely different plans for yourself —
God, or Fate, or The Divine
has a way of showing us what we need.

Your job is to understand that,
be grateful, and continue with that flow.

Intention:
Am I overly critical of how far I have come?
Can I instead look for progress?

## 312. Work For It

*I would prefer this one be wrapped up with pretty language about how "everything is possible if you believe!"*

Unfortunately, we cannot.
Nothing will move forward if you don't push it.
We do not have the ability to make things happen
without doing anything.
No matter what you want to do,
you must do what is required to achieve any goal.
You must 'play the part', so to speak.

Actors have often said that they play the 'money parts',
so they get to play the actual parts they want to play —
This is to say: they take the job that moves them forward
toward their goal, even if it's not 100% what they wanted.

This is true in every aspect of the world.
You cannot make change without first playing the game.
You have to work for the goal, and that includes
doing all of the things that are required.
The magic only happens if you jump through the hoops of life,
if you show up, and if you work for it.

Of course, in a utopia
we would all just get what we wanted
because we dreamt it.

But this is not a utopia,
and we are worth fighting for what we want.

Intention:
Do I do the work?

# You Can Be Free

# 313. Life Is Suffering

*Technically the first noble truth is something like:*
*Life contains suffering, pain and misery.*

Ancient Nepal may have been the first ones
to toss around the meme about
everyone having pain on their Journey.

The great story* goes:
that, around 400 BCE, this disenfranchised frat boy
named Sid dropped his oppressive aristocratic parents' ways,
adopted a completely austere hippie life,
and became enlightened.

He decided to introduce the world to the Eight-Fold Path,
and later became known as the Buddha.

We aren't the first to suffer;
we aren't the only ones suffering;
We can get better.

There are as many ways down the Path
away from suffering, as there are modern fat
and happy depictions of the Buddha.
The first step is to realize we can move
toward enlightenment — or not.

The choice is yours_

Intention:
Do I see that I can choose to move toward more contentment?

*Buddhism is the fourth largest religion in the world. It has an amazing story you may want to explore beyond the tongue-in-cheek description here.

## 314. Breath and Feel Lighter

This is as good a place as any.

Your breath is always with you.
It is a constant companion in times of stress.
Focus in on your breathing
whenever that anxiety starts to take hold.
Know that if you are focusing on your breathing,
you are not focusing on the panic.
Even when it is inconvenient to do anything else,
you have your breathing.

Picture a calm light coming in,
and the toxic waste going out.
Try to picture how this breathing
is scrubbing out your cells,
and adding sparkly happy juice to them!

It is your damn visualization,
you can picture whatever the hell you want!

Practice this simple tool
as often as your heart clenches
or your gut sours.

Intention:
Do I know how to use my breathing to calm myself?

# 315. Have Confidence In The Path

Which Path, again?

Your Path, your Journey.

Will you fall down tomorrow,
and feel crushed under the weight of everything?

Probably not.

But– who Knows?

You certainly don't!

*Why in the world would you waste another minute worrying about it.*

There are an infinite number of possibilities for tomorrow.
You have chosen to walk down this Path,
and, even if you fall, you know you can get back up,
and do what you need to do again.

Right now, right here, own it!

You've totally Got this!

Intention:
Do I understand that I am the only one
who can create true confidence in me?

## 316. Put One Foot In Front Of The Other

Don't overwhelm Yourself.

Confidence continues to build after a series of little successes.
It is impossible to look at every possibility at once.
We bust it down into manageable pieces.
We do one little thing at a time.
We give ourselves credit,
and we move on to the next thing.
We see how the Path will lead us toward our goal.
We don't need all the answers right now.
We just need confidence in ourselves
and faith in our Journey.
Move forward one foot at a time.

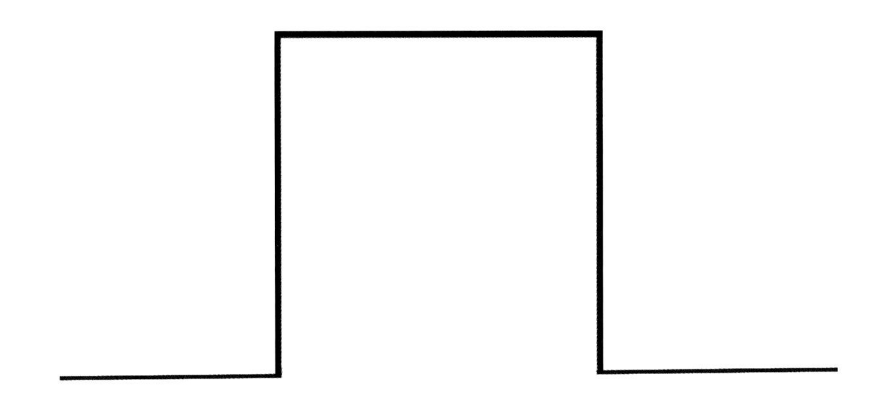

Intention:
Do I take my life one step at a time?

## 317. Keep Your Faith Simple

*"Religion is for people who fear hell.*
*Spirituality is for those who have been there."*
*~Original quote, origin uncertain.*

Belief in *anything* can be trying at times.
Spending a bunch of time defining and defending
what are, essentially, magical beliefs is the opposite of Faith.
If you are a Spiritual person,
this behavior tends to take you away from God,
as it is pretty easy to rip holes in religious beliefs.

Keep your Faith simple;
define it for yourself.

Hold yourself to at least the standard of:
*'do unto others as you would like done unto you.'*

Then, tell anyone else to bugger off!
Faith is for you, and you alone.
You don't need to explain that to anyone —
least of all someone who is going to tell you
why your Spiritual path is wrong.
It is your Journey.

How the hell would they know what's best for you?

Intention:
Do I Believe simply and purely?

## 318. Reject Fundamentalism

*Fundamentalism. destroys faith.*

This is a bit controversial, but it needs to be said.
If we knew who or what God really was, we would be God.

Faith is personal.

It is your personal Journey with belief in something greater than you. For some of you, this is something scientific. For others, this is defined by a religion, or a simple belief in a great spirit or power in the universe.

Fundamentalism destroys original purpose.

Sometimes it is enthusiasm. Usually, it is an amygdala brain response that isn't about teaching and enlightening, but rather an ancient instinctive need to protect the pack.

*This doesn't just apply to religion — but to any organization with a manual.*

Once a belief lands in this part of the brain,
there is a physical response to fight anyone who thinks differently. This isn't logical thinking. We aren't animals. There are many ways to get to a place where your amygdala doesn't run the show.

*You are on the path now!*

We don't care how you get there, just get there.

Intention:
What are the things in my life where I have become fundamentally intolerant? Do I see how irrational a fundamentalist belief is?

## 319. Accept A Bad Day

*Because It Really is Okay—*

The axiom 'tomorrow is a new day' is timeless.
The worst can happen,
and you can still get up the next morning,
look around you, and face it.

Do you have control over a pandemic?
Do you have control over the state of world affairs?
Do you have control over a diagnosis?
Do you have control over other people's decisions?

Arguably, we could say
there are some things listed above that you can control,
but overwhelmingly no.

No, you cannot fix the world.
No, you cannot reverse time, and make this bad day go away.
You cannot change what you,
or the people around you, have already done.
You cannot eliminate the mistake you made.

You can breathe.
Know that tomorrow,
or very soon after, will be better.
You can see that through acceptance,
you are one step closer to being on the other side of this crap.

*You can let it go—*

Intention: Do I let bad things define me?
Do I know how to accept the moment and move on?

## 320. Change It Up

*Don't just suffer through it, see a new way through it.*

See solutions_

Don't sit in misery wondering how things are going to get better.

Start to change it up.

If there are things that you don't like,
take responsibility for yourself
and do something different.
This can be small but revolutionary.

Start to develop the habit
of, when something goes wrong,
looking how to change your circumstances
so that you don't have to live in it.
You can accept bad days, but not a bad life.

No one else is responsible for your
anger, frustration, depression, or misery.
Only you can take the steps to change your world.
The possibilities are endless,
if you allow for your mind to open to them.

Intention:
What can I do to address my own part/role in my problems?

## 321. Look At Yourself

*You are everything you need to be and more!*

Are you the self-critic?
Are you the blamer?
Are you the denier?
Are you a combination of all these things?

There are endless ways our minds
make us deal with our imperfections.
The problem isn't that we *have* imperfections.

*WE ALL DO.*

The problem is in how we respond to ourselves in those moments.
Do we let them crush us?
Do we pretend they don't exist?
Do we see them as everyone else's fault?

We all do some of these things.

Look honestly at yourself. If no one understands you,
you are the blamer. If you don't have any issues, you are the denier.
If you are the cause of every problem, you are the self-critic.

We all have combinations, but we tend to lean toward one of these.
Start to understand, and accept, these things. Understand everyone,
(literally everyone) does these things, so they are absolutely normal.
The difference is that once you identify those things in yourself,
you can work on them.

*You can "see" yourself more clearly.*

Intention:
Do I know how I respond to my imperfections?

## 322. Aerobic Exercise

Because really –
drugs are bad for you.

Drugs and alcohol are fun,
but they really can't be your primary source
of mental health maintenance.
They, essentially, are bad for you.
You know what isn't?
Exercise.

*(Of course, excessive exercise with an eating disorder*
*is a different story, but that isn't this conversation.)*

This is about creating balance in life;
about making sure that you don't drown yourself
in mood altering chemicals, and miss the actual activity of life.
This is about taking thirty minutes
(or more, if you're into that)
to walk, run, or whatever...
rather than five hours to drink the night away.

This is about recognizing health over easy fixes.
This is holistic self-care at its most fundamental level.

Try this route.

Intention:
What do I do to boost the natural
"happy" chemicals in my brain?

## 323. Journal Your Moods

I am PISST OFF
THERE—I journaled a mood.

When you journal your moods,
take note of what you ate that day.
Take note of where you are in your cycle.
Correlate it with the moon if you want!
See what activities you did that day.
Journal good moods this way, not just the bad.

After a while, very distinct patterns will emerge.
Your moods will ebb and flow
according to a thousand different factors.
Understanding yourself is a fundamental part
of being able to deal with yourself.
It is amazing how little we can see ourselves
and our responses in this chaotic life we lead.
Taking a minute to identify how you respond
to food, environment, hormonal cycles, activity,
and even the moon, can help you identify
the things you can change and the things you can't.

Maybe you learn
that eating Ding-Dongs makes you a raging bitch!
Stop eating those everyday if that's the case!
Maybe you learn that two days before your period
you go into a deep depression.

You can emotionally prepare for
those things now!

Intention:
Do I see how my moods are correlated to my life
and the choices I make?

# 324. Tap Into A Vital Force

*"For my ally is the force. And a powerful ally it is. Life creates it, makes it grow. Its energy surrounds us and binds us.*
*Luminous beings are we, not this crude matter."*
*~ Yoda, Empire Strikes Back*

If we are basically an electrical system contained in a body,
then, yes, luminous beings, we are.
We are essentially the ghost in the machine.
Whatever is deep inside you
that allows you to draw strength, reach there.
If it is the Holy Spirit, great!
If it is the neuronal connections that
we don't quite understand yet,
but know exist on some higher level
than we can currently scientifically explain — great!
If it is genetic, ancestral imprinting, tap into that!

We don't care how you define inner strength.
We care that you understand it is a vital force
that is greater than the sum of your parts.

We care that you understand it is bigger than you,
and always there for you.
We care that you learn how to depend
on it for guidance and strength.
It is the subtle difference between a gut reaction,
and really digging deep.
Gut reactions are potentially harmful and just animal instinct.
We are talking about moving with the flow of life.
We are talking about something universal.
Learn how to tap into something greater.

Intention:
Do I see how it is important that I let myself be guided
by something greater than the sum of my own parts?

## 325. You Can Be Free

No Matter where You are -

Moving along the Path
leads to moments of pure, simple, freeing Peace.

All the fighting and suffering is essentially fighting against the Path. When you start to embrace self-care, you get to feel free.

This requires us to say 'yes' to changes in thoughts and behaviors. This is not to say that you need to say yes to doing everything for other people. If we are women, that is what we do anyway.

Yes, to change. Yes, to help. Yes, to health. Sometimes, we are scared. Sometimes, we think it's boring. Sometimes we think we will lose our character when we go down a healthy path. The truth is, we don't get to be anything interesting or cool
until we fix ourselves.

Janis Joplin was "cool", but she was miserable, damaged, and dead by 27. The myth that damaged people are a goal is simply that: a myth. Most of the people that are fascinating are achievers through a combination of healthy collaboration, grit and, yes, a sense of greater purpose.

Getting healthy
(in all aspects of your life, not just in your nutrition)
can free you to become the most incredible you.

Intention:
Do I understand how a foundation of self-care and health
can lead me to becoming an outstanding me?

# Your Attitude Is Your Choice

## 326. If You Are Tired, Understand Why

I am tired every Damn day.

Why are we "tired"?
Is it physical?
Do we get enough sleep;
do we need a good weekend
where we don't get out of bed?
Is it ennui?
Are we bored with the sheer monotony of it?
Are we depressed?
Are we addicted?
Are we one of a thousand other diagnoses?
Are we sick of feeling like this?

Identify what makes you tired.
Refer back to that journal
and see how being tired correlates
with everything else in your life.
Do we need help?
Can we be honest, especially in our minds, about this stuff?
Depression and sleep are practically best friends,
so be sensitive to things like this.
Is there a medical problem?
Look at your life honestly,
and see what is holding you back.
Identify that and address it.

Who has time for nonsense like being tired all the time?

Intention:
What is holding me back?
Can I identify those things that hinder me from being the best me?

# 327. Desire Contentment

Who doesn't?

A lot of us fight happiness.
It is some misguided, protective mechanism that says,
*"Don't let yourself be too happy, that is dangerous!"*
Another reaction is that a person is simple, or weak, or bland
if they are content.

Listen:
people are what they are.
You aren't a boring person,
so why freaking fight happiness?
Why say, 'I'm fine', when you are not?
When you find yourself in a thousand
different states of malcontent,
stop and see why you aren't doing something positive for yourself.

Look at the things in your life that bring you happiness,
and ask yourself why you aren't working towards those things.
If you have given up, readjust your goals.

*Don't throw the baby out with the bathwater.*

You are allowed to adjust.
You are still allowed to fight for happiness
even if your first try didn't work out.
You deserve to be content.

Intention:
Do I really believe that I should be content?

# 328. Cultivate Your Mind

Rolls eyes.

Seriously, this is important.
We really must strive to work our minds throughout life.
This does not include going down
a Facebook echo chamber rabbit hole.

Read, or listen to audiobooks.
Take classes.
Update your mind by listening to professionals
who know more.
Improve your mind.

If you do this regularly,
you can have some solid tools in place for yourself
when memory and critical thinking are a gift rather than a given.
It creates brain muscle memory.
It allows your brain to learn how to adjust as it gets older.

If you are not working to improve the muscle in your head,
you will sink in on yourself over time.
This leads to fear and anxiety;
the real world doesn't stand still like that.

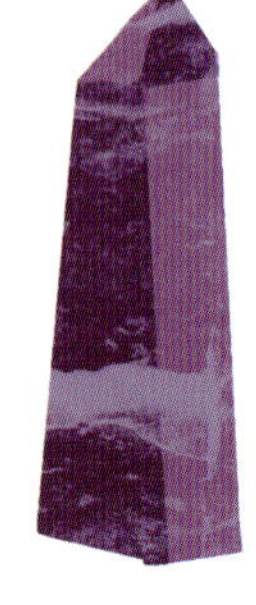

Intention:
What things can you do to improve your mind?

# 329. Dissect Your Character

And– get super comfortable with it.

There is always character work to be done.
This is a huge part of the Journey. Be okay with it.
Look at all the aspects of your personality dispassionately.
There isn't a part of you that is bad or good.

*Just you.*

If something annoys you about yourself,
take a deeper look at it, and see what you can do to change it.

*Be open to that.*

You can move through one thing at a time,
and all of sudden you are evolving into the person you want to be.
This isn't to say that you were awful or bad —
just not finished yet.
And, we are never finished.
Break down those character bits.
Some of them are you to the core.

*Celebrate those.*

Some bits need tweaking. Some need altogether re-vamping.
Make this a part of every Path. It is ongoing work for all of us.

Intention:
Do I recognize aspects of my personality?
Which things should I work on today?

## 330. Desire To Be Better

But I just told you–
I'm tired.

This one is tricky.
We want you to take care of yourself;
we want you to be kind to yourself;
we want you to love yourself.
Truly, we want you to love yourself
more than anyone else.

We want you to love yourself
so that you see that you are worthy enough to be better.
We want you to not put everyone else before you.
If you are in a partnership,
and each of you are working toward being your best you,
you will naturally have the strength
and confidence to support each other.
This is a byproduct of focusing on
your own mind-body-spirit connection.
This is the Foundation of being better.

*Love yourself enough to care for yourself.*

Then you can be strong enough to be there for others.

Intention:
Do I see how loving myself and wanting to make myself better
affects everything and everyone around me?

## 331. Find Some Shiny Star

And be more like her.

When the boredom, depression, and anxiety
of life set in, look around.
Actively find inspiration.
There are superstars in history.
There are superstars in life right now.
There are inspirational characters in books and movies.
Find someone that makes you say,
*'I wish I was more like her'.*
Then, do a few things to make that true.

Actively looking for people to inspire you staves off negativity.
If you are busy focusing on the way
this kick-ass person rocked it out,
it is hard to be depressed or anxious.

Heroes are never perfect in real life,
but we don't need them to be.

*We need them to inspire us to be better.*

Focus on the good things, and work towards those.

Intention:
Who or what can I draw on for inspiration?

## 332. Don't Do Expectations

*The most insulting thing on the planet is to be disappointed in someone.*

Don't lay your expectations on someone else.
That isn't a relationship, *that is abuse.*
Even your children need to find their path.
Guide them, yes, but then let them *be them.*
You are not a judge and jury.
You are also *human*
with a monumental amount of screw ups.

If we spend our days laying out expectations on other people,
we will spend a lot of days being disappointed.

Not only is this a rotten thing to do to other people,
but it is also self-abuse.
How tattered our emotions become
when we invest ourselves
in controlling the behavior of others.

We have zero power over those outcomes.
Our expectations damage our emotional health
as well as our relationships.

Intention:
Do I see how the expectations I put on others hurts me and them?

# 333. Be Kind

*"Think this through with me, let me know your mind.*
*Woah-oh, what I want to know, is are you kind?"*
*~ Jerry Garcia and Robert Hunter*

This is repeated because it is that important.

Kindness is not difficult.
Kindness requires that we step into the shoes
of those around us and truly feel for them.
Kindness is not "being nice". It isn't contrite yes's.
Sincerity is required for kindness.
It heals the giver's soul
much faster then any sort of anti-anxiety pill.

*(However, if you are on medication for any*
*mental-health condition, do not stop.*
*This is not saying medication is unecessary or weak.)*

If we give our kindness to those around us,
we can often feel the healing going on inside us *and* them.
Kindness is a tonic for the world that cannot be underestimated.
Kindness requires a strength of character
that is much greater than the opposite.
Anyone can yell, demand, and throw fits of impatience.
Children do that.
Kindness requires a deeper understanding of the situation at hand.
It is a much more evolved perspective.
It is not reactive.
It is the foundation of *problem solving* and *solutions*.

Intention:
Do I see how kindness is a strength that needs developed?
Do I see how kindness and understanding underpin all solutions?

## 334. Recognize When You Are Pissy

Pissy — I'll show you Pissy.

Kindness is great,
but first we have to recognize our own behavior.
Sometimes we just want what we want.
This is when we have to stop
and take inventory of our behavior.

This guttural, childish response is inherent in all of us,

*so don't feel guilty.*

True happiness comes from a deeper place
than what is essentially a selfish, self-obsessed place.
We must identify the root of our feelings.
Letting go of the need to be right,
or the fear of being wrong may be the first step.
Next, we can look at the other person involved in this moment.
Sometimes, we need to walk away
and figure out our motivation.
Sometimes, we can just reel it in right there
because we see our folly.

The key is to *recognize* our *own* behavior and check it.

Intention:
Do I know when I am *off?*
Do I recognize that the people around me
see me when my emotions come out sideways?

# 335. When Something Really Makes You Angry, It Is Probably You

Nope. I'm pretty sure that bitch really pissed me off.

*No one else is ever responsible for your emotional response.*

No matter what they do.

We are owners of our emotions and responses.
This is why, sometimes, someone can be a total asshole,
and you are virtually unaffected.
You look at them and think,
'that has nothing to do with me'.
When we rage, this is always
(yes, always) about us, not them.
This is complicated to sort out.

With family, there are often lifelong feelings of hurt, pain, guilt,
and obligation tied up in those responses.
Emotions like feelings of inadequacy
can lead to political rage.
Control issues and jealousy are common at work.
The point is, we are harboring some deeper response
that is about us, not them.
Frequently these feelings are irrational,
and once we sort them out we can let them go.
You feel guilty about not calling your abusive relative
because #society. It makes you rage against them.
But once you identify that feeling guilty
is not a rational response when creating healthy boundaries,
you aren't so full of rage.
Pull the rage out and look at it.
It's the only way.

Intention:
Do I harbor rage?
What is it about that rage that I need to sort out?

## 336. Happiness Is Like A Love Drug

Straight from the desk
of the Mayo Clinic.

The Mayo clinic reports on their website,
*"Stress relief from laughter? It's no joke".*
After you are done groaning and hopefully chuckling,
the article goes on to attribute a myriad of short term
and long term health benefits to laughter.
Things like boosting your immune system,
relaxation, pain relief and personal satisfaction.

Think about this.

Let's be happy.

Let's prefer happiness to being/feeling right.
Let's embrace the idea that we can be content
without needing to ride anyone else down.
Let's find that place of joy
and access that, rather than drugs or other abusive tendencies.

Let's choose happiness over
all the other choices.

Intention:
Do I choose happiness over my ego?
Do I see what happens when I don't?

## 337. It's Imperative To Be Positive

Even when it seems impossible
find some joy.

For this Journey,
wouldn't it be a bit easier if we embraced a little positivity?
When we are truly positive, we see solutions — not problems.
We see possibilities not barriers.
We see change as moving forward, not frightening.
We see differences as adding to our lives rather than threatening.

We see the whole damn world
as something worth being a part of.
It may sound a little dramatic,
but this perspective allows
for that beautiful, simple feeling of compassion
to seep right down into your soul.

Without an understanding of what a positive attitude is,
we can't see a way out of our problems.
The world could use a little more of this perspective.

Intention:
Do I see how a positive attitude toward my life
can open doors to solutions?

## 338. Your Attitude Is Your Choice

Remember to work on the things. You can change—

We are all hard-wired a little one way or the other.
But, that is no excuse for bad behavior and negative attitudes.
Our perspective of the world can change,
but we must be willing.

We can choose to live in suffering,
or we can take a look at things,
and bit-by-bit create a life that we want.
This starts with the attitude that you can, in fact, do this.
You have the choice to see the solutions.

Sometimes we are scared.
Sometimes we honestly don't want to face the work.
Sometimes we have convinced ourselves of failure.

Those are *perspectives*, not truths.

Your attitude is your choice.
Make this your mantra.

Intention:
Your attitude is your choice.

# The World Is Your Stage

## 339. Love Yourself Enough To Risk It

*"Just try new things. Don't be afraid.*
*Just step out of your comfort zones and soar."*
*~ Michelle Obama*

Somewhere along the way,
someone convinced us that we weren't worthy
of taking that Chance.
That Chances were for other people.
That we are not good enough to take that Risk.

What do we know by now though-?

Yep, tell that bitch to "Shut Up!"
No one is going to make things happen in your life for you.
You must take the risk; whatever that may be.
Hurdle over the thing that is blocking you from being you.
Take the Risk and know you can jump high enough.
What do you do when you fall?

Yes Girl! You get back up.

That is loving yourself fiercely,
and that is what this Journey is about.

Intention:
What is blocking me from taking a risk in my life? Why?

# 340. Find Your Beauty

*"Everything has beauty, but not everyone sees it."*
*~ Confucius*

Everything has beauty. Everything.
Find your beauty. We can love ourselves completely.

Allow yourself to feel beautiful.

This isn't to say that you need to have surgery,
and plasticize yourself into a life size Barbie doll.
But rather this is to say:
find out what makes you feel beautiful and do that.
Be okay with exploring this side of you.
Be okay with risking it.
And this is the most important part: Do it only for yourself.
No one can take away a beauty that you feel…
Not without your permission, anyway.
This is a little kindness to yourself.
Allow yourself to feel special, just for You.

Wear that Necklace -
buy the Boots -
Rock that Dress
Put the makeup on
or take the makeup off -

Do the things that make you feel beautiful.
Then rock out to the street like a phoenix,
every damn day.

Intention:
Do I allow myself to feel beautiful?

## 341. Prioritize Self-Love

*No one else will love you the way you can love yourself.*

No one knows what you truly want on the inside.
No one else knows you like you do.
No one is going to be able to care
for you the way that you do,
so, make that your first priority.
Love the shit out of yourself!
Love yourself more than enough.
This doesn't mean to become a megalomanic
who has zero consideration for anyone else.

This is the kind of love that oozes out of your pores,
and into other aspects of your life.
This is love that allows you to have
an inner strength that you can give others —
sometimes just by being a living example.

This is a self-love that is born of humility and gratitude.

That type of self-love is enduring.

Intention:
Do I know how to love myself with great compassion?

## 342. Figure Out Who You Want To Be

And change it up- Anytime you want.

Sometimes on our Path
we fall into a pattern.
We decided we wanted to be or do something
and then, ten years later,
it is defining every bit of who we are.
We don't have to be what we do.

We aren't mothers, first. (Scandalous Right?)

We are people who have children. We are that person, first.

We aren't physicians or administrative assistants.
We are people who do these things.
We can be anyone we want.

Start by defining who you want to be.
Do you want to be a person who is caring,
compassionate, and classy?
Or…do you want to be a person
who is intellectual, inspiring, and sassy?

You need to know who you want to be
and what is important to you.

Intention:
Have I looked at what kind of person I am?
Is that who I want to be?

## 343. Be That Person

Okay - right. Just like that?

This will probably take some practice.
You need to picture who you want to be.

What does that person even look like?
What are their priorities?

How do they interact with others?

At first this will seem fake.
But like the sorting hat told Harry Potter:

*"You get to choose who you are."*

There is no shame with turning your
Slytherin tendencies into Gryffindor.

Have some faith
that you can do what you need to do
in order to become the person you want to be.

Intention:
Do I see how I can practice becoming the person I want to be?

# 344. Take Feedback

*The ballerina teacher says, "You are fat and lazy and you need to put your shoulders back". Don't listen to what is unnecessary. What you hear from now on is just 'put your shoulders back'*

Listen to what someone is saying without hearing hate.
Many times, a person is simply giving you their expertise, but all we hear is criticism. This is likely because, in our past, someone was not very good at doing this.

The problem with feedback, is that it is often wrapped in unnecessary criticism, and it seems like a personal attack.

Most of the time this kind of feedback is lost because of the emotional response it causes in us. Feedback from all aspects of life is important so that we can learn and move forward. Start the practice of discerning feedback.

Is the person an expert?
What useful thing are they saying?
Can I learn from that and understand that this sad, unhealthy person really needs to get on their own Path?
Can I take the feedback without the emotional baggage?

Not always easy to do.
Our egos are fragile little eggs.

Practicing this will allow us to become strong over time.
It may lead us to surpass the sad person with all the self-esteem issues. Then you can model the Path of compassion and guidance for them.

Intention:
Do I take feedback?
Or do I immediately think someone is calling me stupid?
Am I okay with not knowing something?

## 345. Put In The Effort

All good things require patience & effort.

So often we want things to happen *now*.
We start and quit instead of start and fall.
We see the Goal, and not the Journey.

*But we don't know how to stop this pattern.*

Just do the things, even on the days we gift ourselves
with a Netflix binge or some such —
do one thing.

It can be just five minutes to further a goal,
but it reminds you that everyday
we have to try just a little to stay on this Path.
This is not to say beat yourself to a pulp, so you just quit again.
Just remind yourself every day that you are on this Path,
and remind yourself where you are in your Journey.
That way when/if you fall,
you don't see things as insurmountable.
You know you can restart with
five minutes of stair walking.
You can take just one class this semester.
You can write one page.
You can meditate.
You can pray
(or simply talk to a lost loved one).
You can forgive yourself, and restart.
Put the effort in, just a little, every day
so that life is easier when the going gets tough.

Intention:
Can I do just a little every day to move me along my Path?

# 346. Walk With Confidence

*Fake it 'til you make it.*

You can't be perfect at something
you aren't doing regularly.
You won't be a master for a while.
Whether it's just being a confident person,
or some more specific goal like owning that bakery.

The point is, you can start trying.
Own that Path and walk with the
Confidence of someone who is full of self-love,
who is putting in the effort
and who knows how to get back up.
You cannot lose if you don't give up.
You can adapt and change,
but this is your path and as long you stay on it,
you are winning.

Remember the "winning" is simply part of the Journey.
The destination isn't the Journey.

Keep moving.
Keep walking.
Keep your head high.

Intention:
Can I dig into that inner confidence today?

## 347. You Can Learn Unexpected Things

*And I wonder looking at the rain, how much thunder can turn the sky to flame? ~ Patti Griffin*

Sometimes, when we are going along a Path,
we begin to change the way we Think.
This can be frightening.
We start to shift our belief paradigms.

This is natural when you think about it.

If what we know got us to a place where we are stuck,
and now we are moving toward a healthier place,
we are likely going to be thinking a little differently.
If your previous way of thinking
is what got you stuck in the first place,
maybe it is time to let it go.

Embrace a new way.

Let yourself learn new, unexpected, exciting things
that help you become your best you.

Intention:
Are you learning new things? Are you allowing yourself to do this?

## 348. Build A Better Self-Image

*"We can rebuild her. We have the technology."*
*~ The Bionic Woman*

Bit-by-bit, you get to remake who you are.
You get to re-envision who you want to be.
You get to define your faith and your beliefs.
No one else gets to do
any of these things for you anymore.
You can do them yourself.
The benefit of this is that
you get to start Celebrating yourself.

You Kick Ass.

You are amazing and you are sure as shit
silencing that bitch in your head.

This is the jumping off point
where you leave that girl from before behind,
and hail the person you are becoming.

Intention:
Can you take the leap and celebrate who you are today?

## 349. Say "Thank You" More And "Sorry" Less

I'm sorry, I do that all the time.

Can we, right now,
completely obliterate the practice
of apologizing for our very existence?

How about saying, "Great, I can do that. Thanks for the feedback"
or 1,000 other variations of acknowledgement?
This goes right along with understanding
that feedback is not criticism.
We don't need to ask forgiveness for not knowing something.
That is silly, we don't know it. It isn't our fault.
Someone can help you along your way with their guidance.
We don't need to apologize to them, we need to thank them.

*Yes, even when they are an asshole.*

Maybe the assholes don't get the "thank you",
but they are the ones that you better not
be apologizing to anymore!

That shit just perpetuates this idea of being sorry for existing.
Assholes are why we feel the need to apologize all the time.
Stop giving them what they think they deserve.
Give that love to yourself.

Intention:
Do I apologize too much?

## 350. Be Unapologetically You

*Know you are completely who you are supposed be.*

This starts at the lunch table at school.
When a kid says something like, "Ewwww, that's gross,"
as you are about to bite into your totally awesome
liverwurst sandwich.
Well, news flash: We aren't 8 years old anymore
and adults who behave like that are small-minded assholes.

Furthermore—They can Suck it!

But since we are a loving, compassionate folk,
we don't actually say that to them.
Instead, we own ourselves with the confidence
we have learned and say,
"I flippin love liverwurst".
Or frilly shirts.
Or science fiction.
Or lime green cabinetry.
Or lavender in your chili.
Or whatever it is.

People cannot hurt you with their opinions or words
unless you give them that power over you.

Laugh at their ignorance
over how other worldly good liverwurst is.

It's their Loss.

Intention:
Do I let other people tell me how to feel about myself?

# 351. The World Is Your Stage

*"A man who limits his interests, limits his life."*
*~ Vincent Price*

Look around you,
and drop every self-imposed boundary
you have placed on yourself.
See every single possibility as yours.
See the world and its opportunities,
and see yourself within that world.
There are no limits.
There are only the limits you place on yourself.
When opening the package of your life,
there is always a way— no matter what type of box it is in.
Sometimes you just need a box cutter,
and sometimes you need three sharp instruments and a hammer.

The only thing you have to do
is choose how you want to live your life.
Nothing is insurmountable.
Nothing is out of reach.
Just start down that Path.

Intention:
Do I place limits on myself?

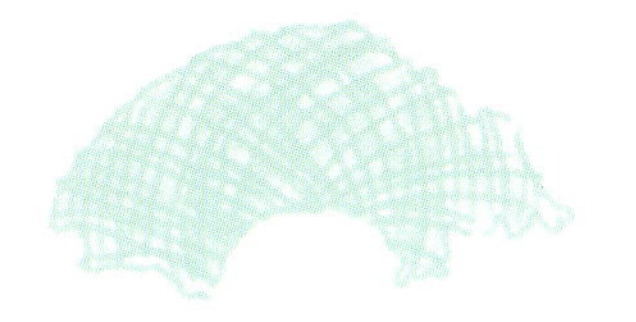

# Be The Change

# 352. Shine For Yourself

*"Never dull your shine for somebody else."*
*~ Tyra Banks*

There are not enough words
to describe how damaging the outside world
can be to your self-esteem.
The best thing to do with that information
is deny the world access to define you.
You can be who and what you want.

Limits are for people who don't have a plan.

This is your Path,
your Journey
and no matter what phase of life you are in,
no one else gets to define it for you.

You shine on for yourself.

This is exciting!
This is life!
This is the Path!

Intention:
Can I define who and what I am just for myself?

# 353. Hit The World Running And Sleep When You Die

*I am not sure this is sound advice.*

Okay, maybe not every day.
Practice seeing your life this way.
See the challenges as exciting.
Be excited that you have so many places
to build yourself up from.

Don't let the day-to-day get under your skin.

Create excitement in your life.
Imagine what you can do
in a 24-hour period
and be amazed by that.
Every once in a while, do just a little more than you think you can.
Stretch your boundaries.

This develops stamina and grit.

Just do it.

Intention:
Do I know how to stretch my capacity?
Can I get excited about that?

## 354. Define What Is Important To You

*All the antioxidants: Chocolate, Wine and Blueberries.*
*I'm going to live forever, Goddammit.*

Okay, antioxidants are important,
but we are thinking more along a philosophical level.
Like what are the things that make your life meaningful?
Try not to default to what you think you should say.

As women, we are frequently told that the most important
thing in our lives is our children.
This is true, but then they grow up and eventually leave.

How about if we don't have any children,
and have no intention of having any?
Where are we, as women, then?

No matter what we say about family,
it cannot be the only thing on our list.
This will bury us in a world that sucks us dry
of our own identity,
and frankly doesn't teach our daughters how to soar.

Who are you without this identity?
What things in life help define you?
What are you passionate about?
What do you like to explore?
What creative outlets do you have?

Look at Yourself & Own it Girl!

You deserve your own truth

Intention:
Have I really looked at who I am, and what I believe?

# 355. Ask For Guidance

*Ask in a thousand different ways.*

We all need a Foundation in some form or another.
This is the strong place that we can turn to
when we don't know what to do next.
Often, this Foundation is situational…
For example, if we are moving somewhere
and we already know someone who lives there.

This is a place and time to ask for guidance.
But also, there is that spiritual ask.
We can ask for inner peace
so that the Path becomes more clear.
This can be done through prayer and/or meditation.
Asking for guidance can become that habit
that you turn to every time you feel you don't know.

Turn outward so that you can better look inward.
Let the answers come and trust the process.

Trust the Guidance.

Intention:
Do I know how to seek guidance in my life?

## 356. Set Standards For Yourself

Don't go to Florida for a guy they call
Bullshit Dave!

If no one tells you,
please know you are so much better
than Bullshit Dave.
If Bullshit Dave isn't your particular problem,
look at other areas in your life
where you are blind to the standards you deserve.

Do we let ourselves be treated poorly at work?
Do we allow our family to walk all over us?
Do we say yes to everything, overwhelming ourselves?
By our general disregard of standards for ourselves
we show everyone that we aren't worth it.

Move on to a place
where you are the most important piece
of *your* equation.

Intention:
Are there parts of my life where I don't take care how I am treated?
Do I need some hard and fast boundaries?

# 357. Stand Up for Someone Who Can't Speak For Themselves

*People love to say, "Give a man a fish, and he'll eat for a day. Teach a man to fish, and he'll eat for a lifetime." What they don't say is, "And it would be nice if you gave him a fishing rod." That's the part of the analogy that's missing."*
*~ Trevor Noah*

As we get more empowered,
the way we keep that empowerment is to give a little away.

Are all the gals being mean to someone at work?
Stand up for her.

Is there someone in the neighborhood that is being excluded?
Invite her.

Just like you on your Journey, other people need support.
Other people need to be empowered.
Other people have suffered because of their circumstances.

People don't magically learn to fish;
they can't if they don't even have a rod.

Help them out.
This, invariably, reinforces your own courage.

Intention:
Do I see how helping others
become empowered, helps me?

## 358. Go To A March

*Is this a metaphor?*

No, really.
At least once in your life, attend a gathering
with people who are fighting for something that you believe in.
(Even if everyone else in your world feels differently.)

Check out what all the fuss is about.

If you are already prone to this behavior,
take it to the next level—
volunteer, fundraise, donate, organize, etc.

We need to grow within our beliefs.
Finding others who feel the same
helps build our self-esteem and confidence.

Within this echo chamber, however,
remember to be a voice of compassion.
Remember not to lose yourself to hatred.
This will undo so much of the work you have done.

Work for change with compassion.

Those are not only the real revolutionaries,
they are the most effective.

Intention:
Can I do anything about my concerns in the world?

## 359. Don't Let Memes Drive Your Beliefs

*A meme isn't the truth; a tweet isn't the truth.*

It is a post that is telling you what you already believe,
usually in a ridiculously undocumented and exaggerated frame.
If there are facts or statements — double check them.

Memes and tweets are the single most
corrupt form of information dispersion.
If we are concerned about "the media"
but completely immune to the fact that
most of our information
comes in the form of Facebook memes or Tweets,
we really need to rethink our information paradigm.

Besides, this kind of information tends to be toxic for the soul.
If you want real information, it is generally boring.
It requires processing and thinking
which you are allowed to do for yourself.
Good news, however, processing through the info
is a great confidence builder.

We do love a good hilarious meme.
We just don't give them credence when it comes to our beliefs.

Intention:
Do I depend on social media for my beliefs?

## 360. Don't Take Yourself Too Seriously

EVER – (see what we did there?)

The world turns, the seasons change, empires come and go.

We cannot make change
on a personal or global level
if we walk around halfcocked and ready to blow.
This life is a marathon and the evil that exists today
will still be there tomorrow.
Guarantee it.

We can make a difference over time in our lives,
and, if we are lucky, in the lives of others.
We can only do that if we learn to walk joyfully forward.
Otherwise, the gravity of our fight will overwhelm us.

Emma Goldman, a political activist from the early 20th century,
famously said that she was admonished for dancing as an activist,
which led to the saying,

*"If I can't dance, I don't want to be part of your revolution".*

Dance, laugh, and be a part of it all.
We get one shot at this life.
Be grateful so that we can laugh.

Intention:
Do I take myself too seriously?

## 361. Other People May Disagree

*Listen to them.*

But Good Lord, that can be really hard to do.
We don't suggest subjecting yourself to the ravings
of a lunatic, hate driven, conspiracy theorist
spouting off "the world is ending" rhetoric.

The amygdala will go into full blown
"protect your people" mode and you won't hear a thing.
But, when the opportunity to engage someone
that thinks differently exposes you to the intellectual
and emotional drive behind their beliefs,
it helps us to see solutions.
It helps us creatively address problems.

The problem is never just that those people are stupid.
Or those people are lazy.
Or those people are any single adjective.
The problem is that those people are
disenfranchised and unempowered.
If we learn this common ground, we can start to see
some answers to these problems. Hear our own fear
when we have these conversations and squash that down.
Fear is never a good force for change.
Compassion is how we make lasting change.
History always bears this out.

Intention:
Do I have enough compassion to hear the other side?

## 362. Don't Be A Hypocrite

When You are wrong – Admit it.

Consistency of belief, and hence fluidity, is really important
in order to not be trapped by our own thinking.
If you can't resolve a topic, choice, or concept
because it goes against your foundational beliefs,
then you have to change the way you think about these things.

This, of course, is presuming that your foundational
beliefs are immutable items like:

*"do unto others as you would have them do unto you."*

These things are the moral foundation of any society
that lives within a social system that has evolved
past basic primitive protection and needs.

Let's say something "feels" like it would line up with your principles
because a certain group of people (your family or friends) believe it,
but when you look more closely at it,
you can see it goes against all of your foundational beliefs.

Really gets ya thinking, huh.

You have to change the way you feel
because you are *allowed* to change the way you feel.

Open your Mind. Give yourself permission to Open Your Mind.

Intention:
Do I see how feeling something does not make it true or right?

## 363. Check Your Gut Reaction

*Sometimes my gut tells me to never leave the house or get out of bed - ever again.*

See!
Your gut lies to you.
Trust that your gut reaction is only relevant
to the muscle and the sensory memory
of any given situation.
Trusting our gut to interpret new situations
will not give us accurate information.
Our gut is where we feel fear,
and that is going to lead us to some crazy-ass choices every time.
Fear driven choices, beliefs, and reactions steer us away
from a place where we can make rational helpful decisions.
Gut reactions are great for recognizing that guy
isn't from our pack and may be here to attack us.
Super useful 10,000 years ago in some pre industrial existence.
Hopefully we have evolved past the need to fear those different
from us. But our brains are still made this way,
so we have to be conscious of this.
When we dig deeper, we can connect with something more.
Something that replaces that primitive brain.
Something that connects us with true compassion rather than fear.

This spiritual reality is a much
greater problem solver than the gut.

Look to something greater than the gut reaction
to drive your beliefs.

Intention:
Do I have something to connect to spiritually
that can guide me away from fear?

## 364. Love First and Last

*"Hate generalizes. Love specifies."*
*~ Robin Morgan*

It is so easy to hate everyone,
or an entire group.
It is hard to love everyone,
because there always seems to be that one damn person
who ruins it for the rest.

So, when people speak out about beliefs
that you don't necessarily agree with,
it is easy to categorically hate them
and bunch them in with everyone else.
We don't believe they have anything different to say,
because we have already decided to hate them.

Love them enough to listen.
Then, when they say something you hate,
love them anyway.
You will ultimately win if you look at the world this way.
You get to feel love and compassion
which grow your mind and heart.
Other people can hate across the board,
you can be the one who loves across the board.

Intention:
Can I really try to love someone really different than me?

## 365. Be The Change

Ghandi was Really on to something there.

When you look around you and feel empowered
and you feel nothing but love for you and everyone else,
then you are truly on the Path. You get to be an example to the world; to demonstrate to others how to be feet first on the Journey. You don't have to teach them how to be better.

Its much more simple than that.

You get to show them they can choose to make changes for themselves. They can embrace those changes no matter who they are. You (yes, you yourself) get to illustrate through your own personal Journey how to move through life, and truly learn to love it. If you are lucky, you are connected to something bigger than you.

You get to give back this gift of freedom, compassion, and love to everyone you meet simply by being the change you want to see.

You can still cuss. (Just don't cuss *at* someone).
You can still fall. (Just don't *stay* down)

This is essential for moving forward.
And you can always change up your Path if you need.

What comes next?

The Journey is yours, and you get to choose which Path you are on. Choose wisely, or don't. But walk with confidence onto the next trail, because you cannot fail.

Intention:
Can I take today and celebrate myself and my Journey?

# Now What?

Now you are perfect!

Ba ha ha ha ha!

No, No, we jest.

But now…
Now we keep doing the things.
This little list is infinite.
The multi-headed beast that is life rears its head with change and challenge every damn step of the way.
Personally, this stuff is eternal and bears repeating.

Stay open.
Read it again.
Read it as a bedside daily reader.
Use the app in your car.
Look for other dailies!
Ask other people for advice on what to read.
Commit to this amazing journey
called life and start down your Path.

# About The Gnostic Sentries

*Author - Suzie Newell*

Suzie Newell has her doctorate specializing in coping mechanisms for women with substance use disorder. Her work as a nurse anesthesiologist on obstetric units in the epicenter of the opioid crisis exposed her to the day-to-day roadblocks people face not just within the world of substance use disorder, but in everyday life as well. Her own journey began with a degree in political science working in social justice. Suzie has always championed people's journeys. While in Guatemala during the 500 Years of Resistance campaign, she met a woman who inspired her to return to school and ultimately work in anesthesia. This all sounds perfect on paper, but along the journey she lost half her family, lost a good portion of her mind, and fell down hard. She was lucky enough to get back up, and then get back up again. The work put into developing the Path 365 is the culmination of a lifetime of work in health care, in peer support and within her own personal journey. Sharing this work through a daily direction book is an honor.

*Creative Director and Assistant Editor- Madeline Jaina*

Madeline Jaina is a Nashville based musician, yogi, writer, and generally nice person. They received their BFA in acting from The New School for Drama. As an early talker, Madeline is never short on things to say, words to sing, and opinions to share.

*Editor - Mac Craighead*

Mac Craighead is a Brooklyn-based writer, editor, and all-around good guy. They received their B.F.A. in Drama with a concentration in playwriting from The New School, and are currently writing a cookbook for people who want to feed their super picky, wonderful partners.

*Illustration - Frankie Terrone*

Frankie Terrone is a queer artist and Native New Yorker. Born and bred in South Brooklyn, they are prone to pronounce "coffee" like "caw-fee" or, "dog" like "dawg". Frankie received his BFA from Pratt Institute in 2015, but more importantly they are a Cancer Sun, Pisces Moon, and a Scorpio Rising who loves video games & cartoons.

*Assistant Editor - Matthew Vonderlin*

Matt Vonderlin is an audio engineer, musician, and a connoisseur of beans (coffee and refried) based in Nashville, TN. They received a B.S. from SUNY Fredonia, where they studied sound engineering. They are currently working on producing music for an album to be released this year.

*Assistant Editor - Steve Seccombe*

Steve Seccombe is a heterosexual white guy in power who we allowed on this project because he is also a bad ass feminist, a remarkably kind man and the life partner of Suze. Aside from being able to do virtually anything after reading a manual, Steve has an attention to detail that makes him really annoying at times, and super useful on a project like this. When he is not being an amazing life partner, he's running a manufacturing shop, watching or reading science fiction, gaming, feeding the wildlife, being humble and taking care of others. Often, you can find him walking around generally disappointed in the patriarchy. Really, if you are a heterosexual white guy in power, be more like Steve.